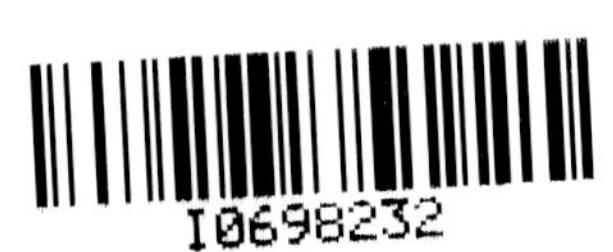

This book belongs to:

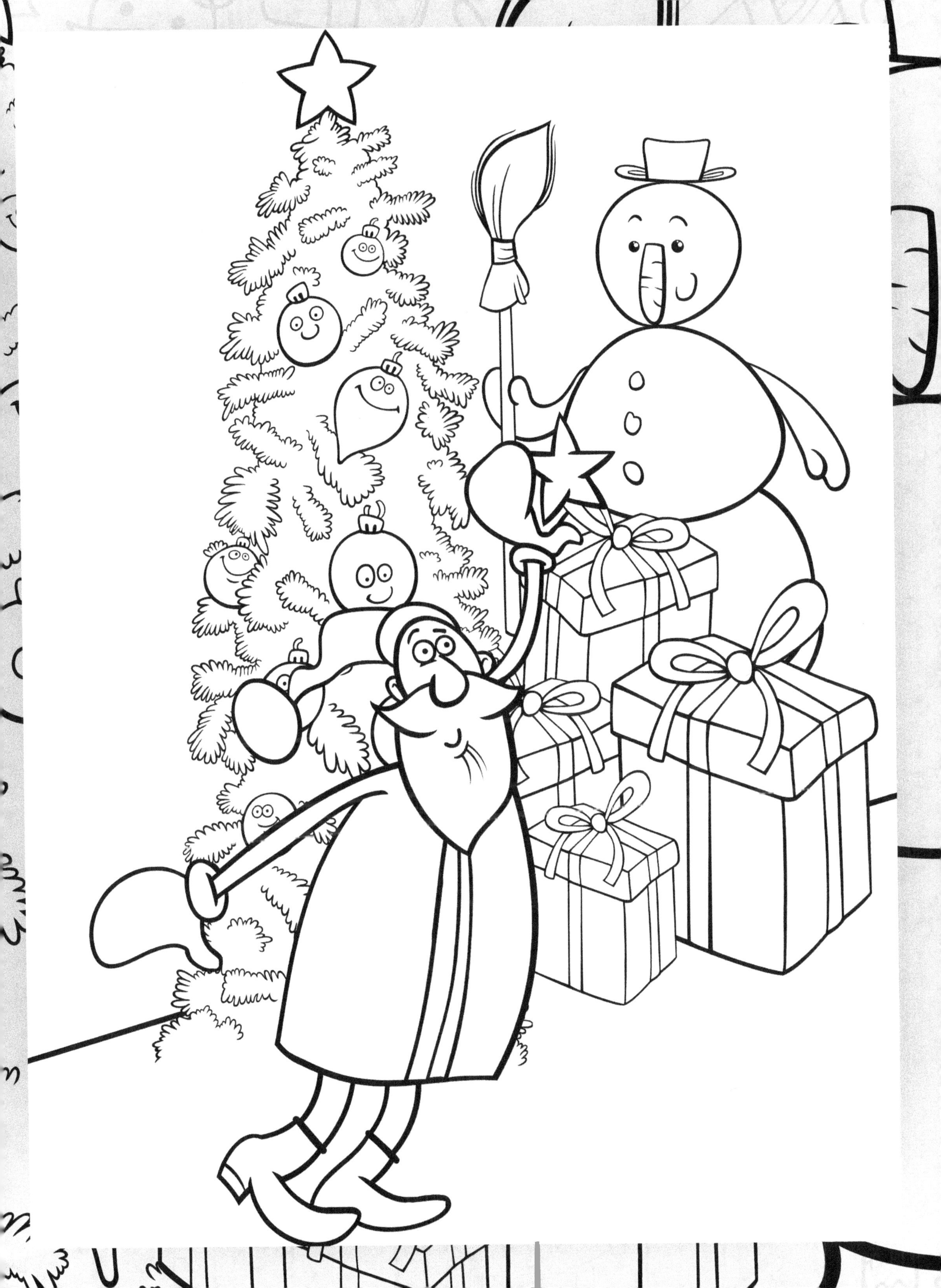

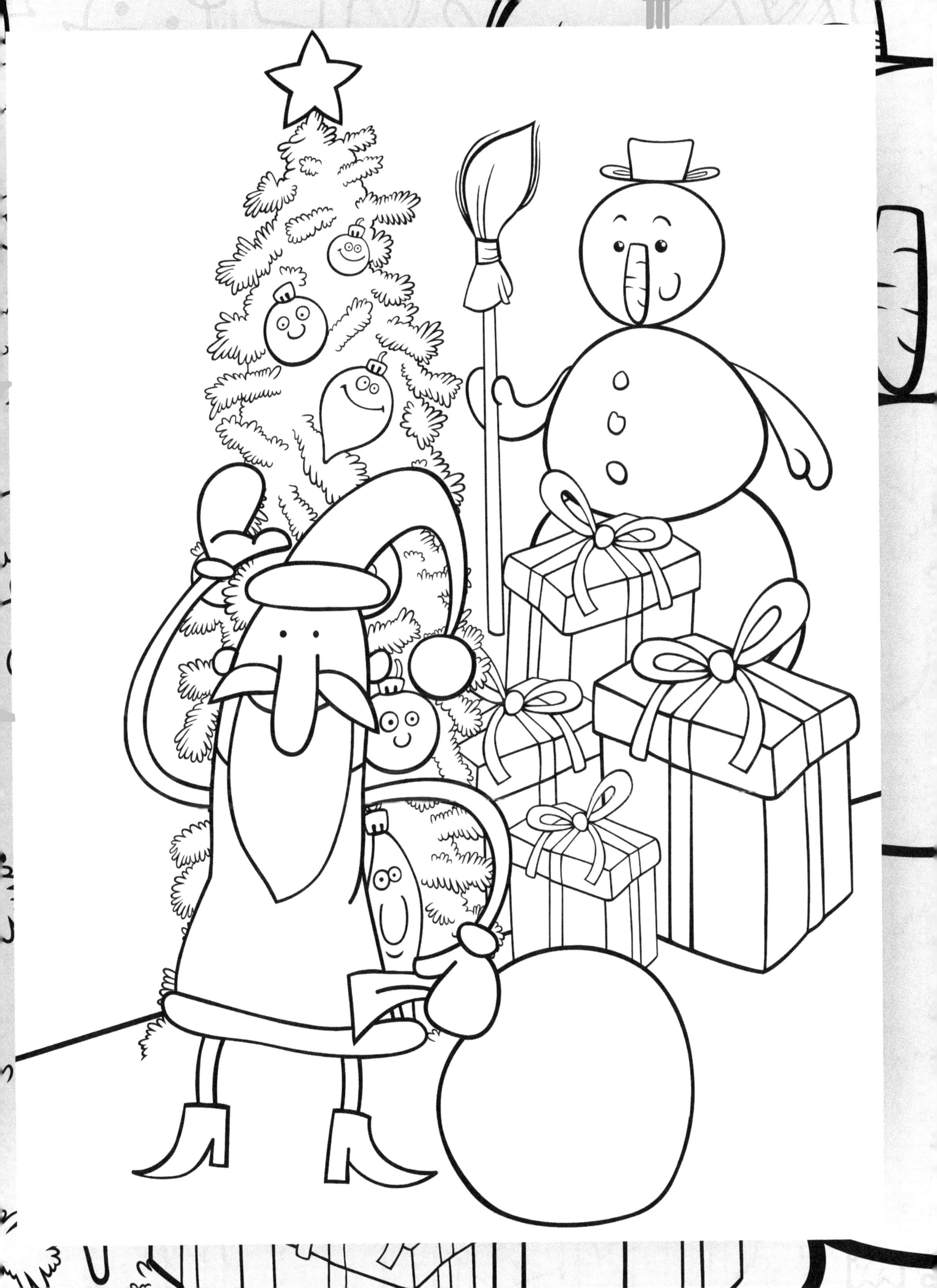

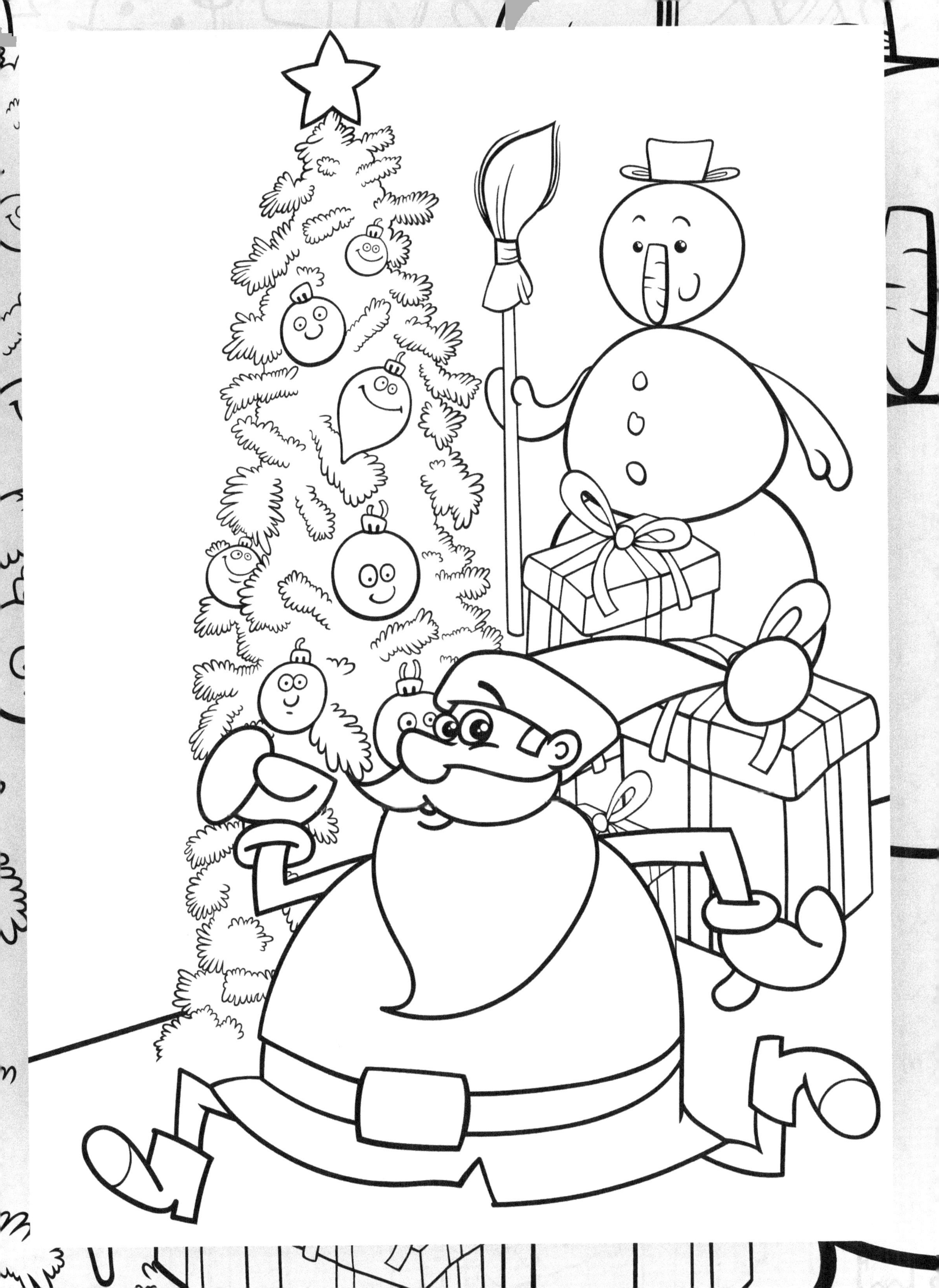

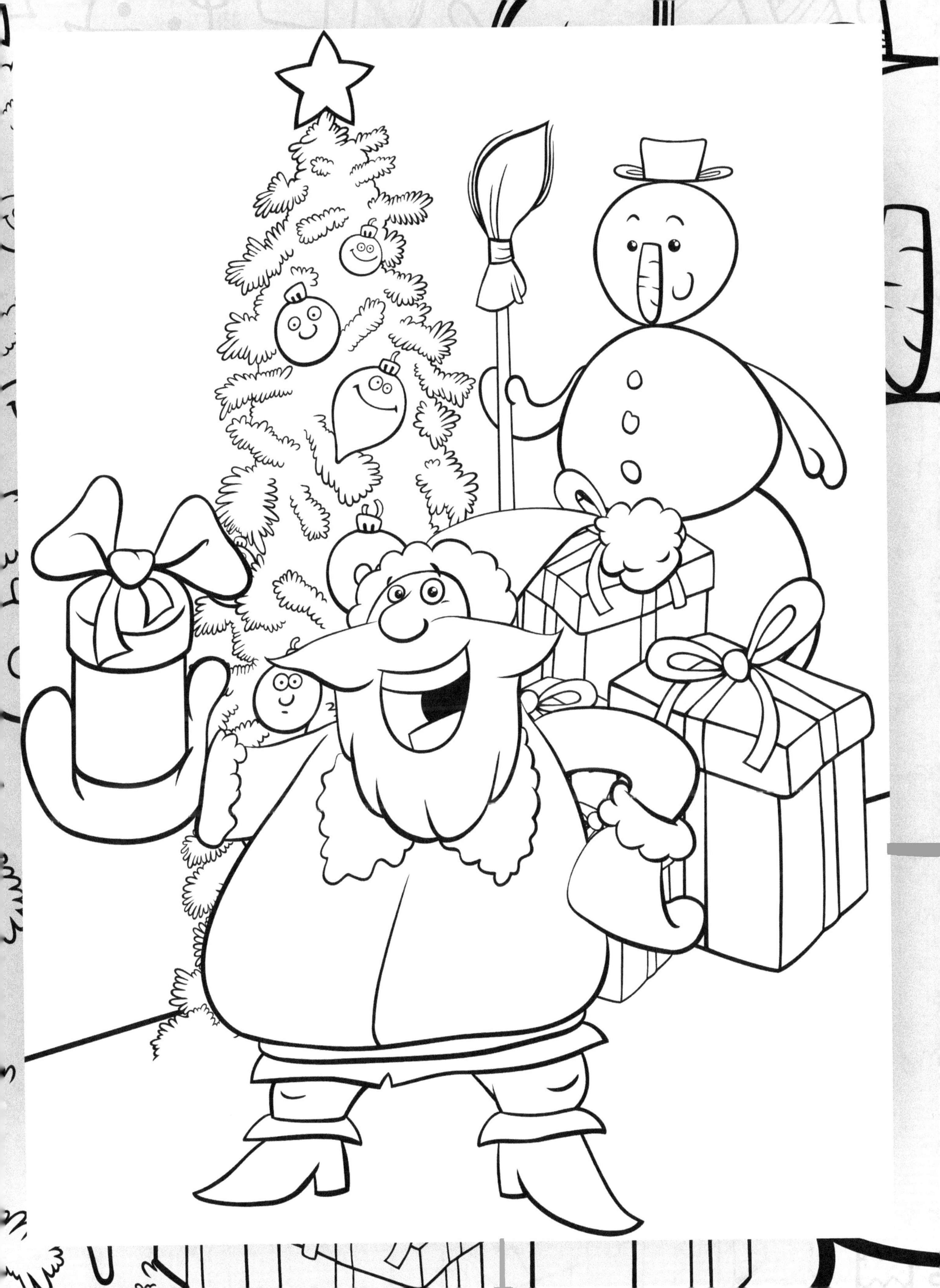

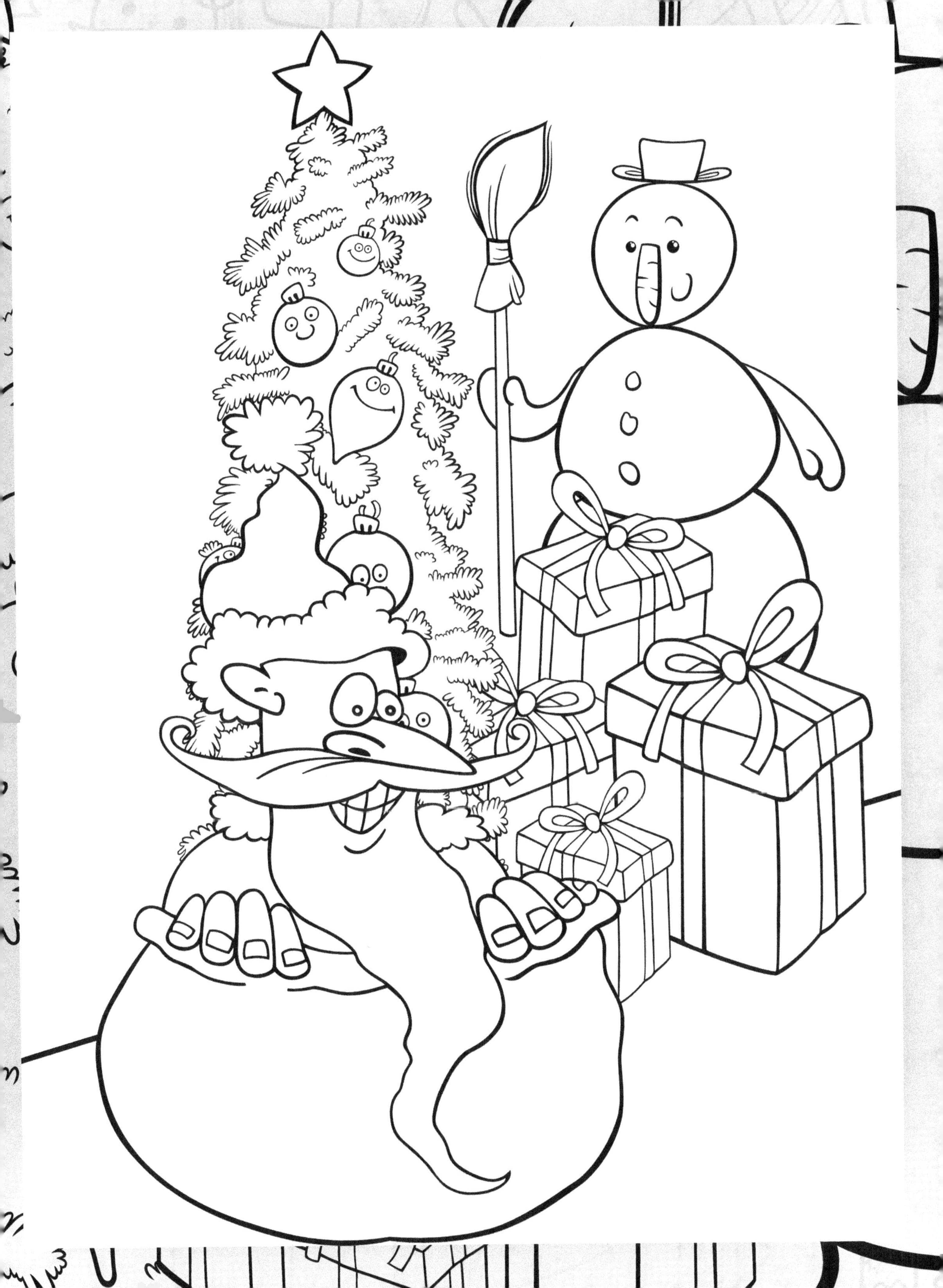

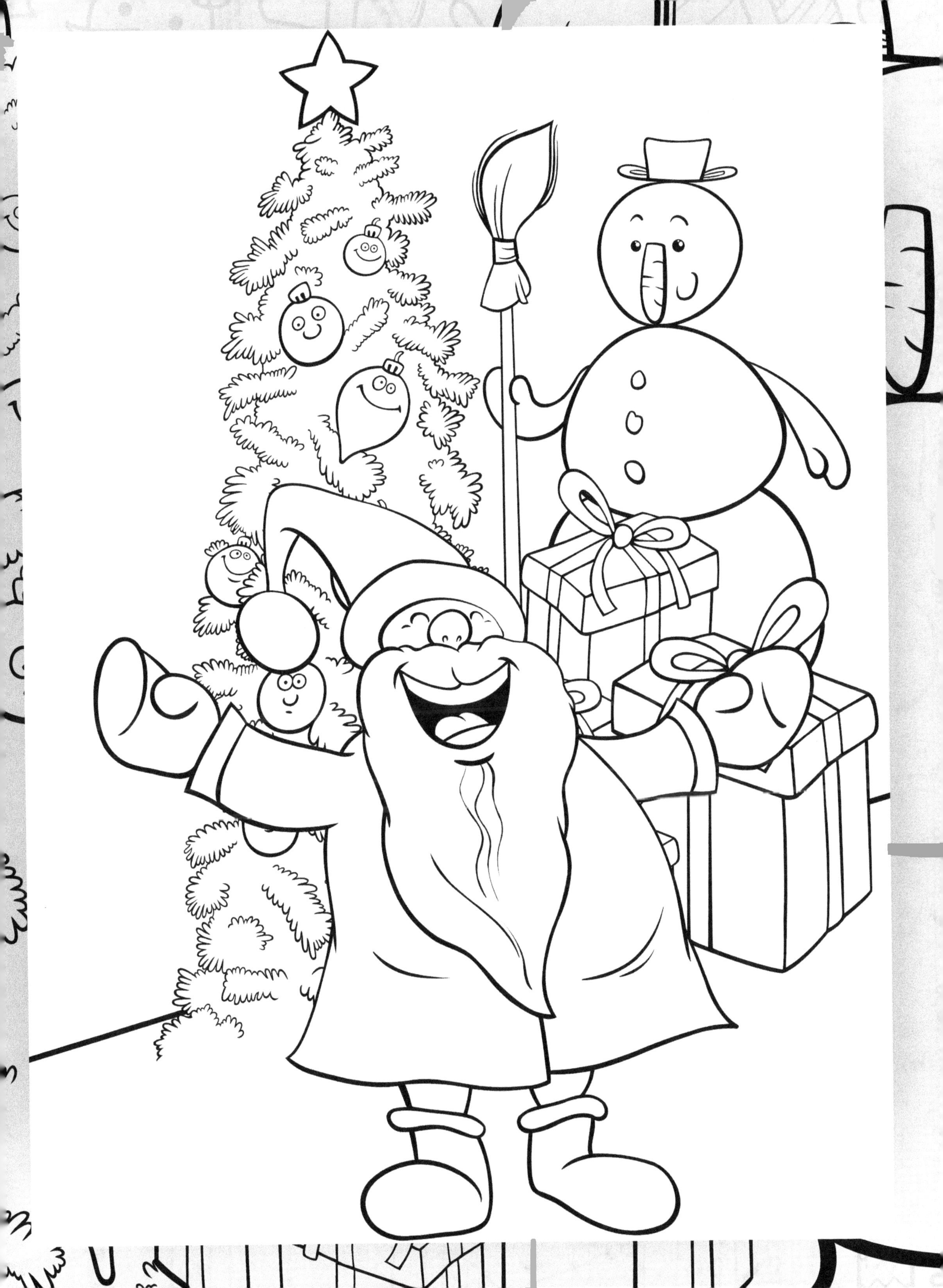

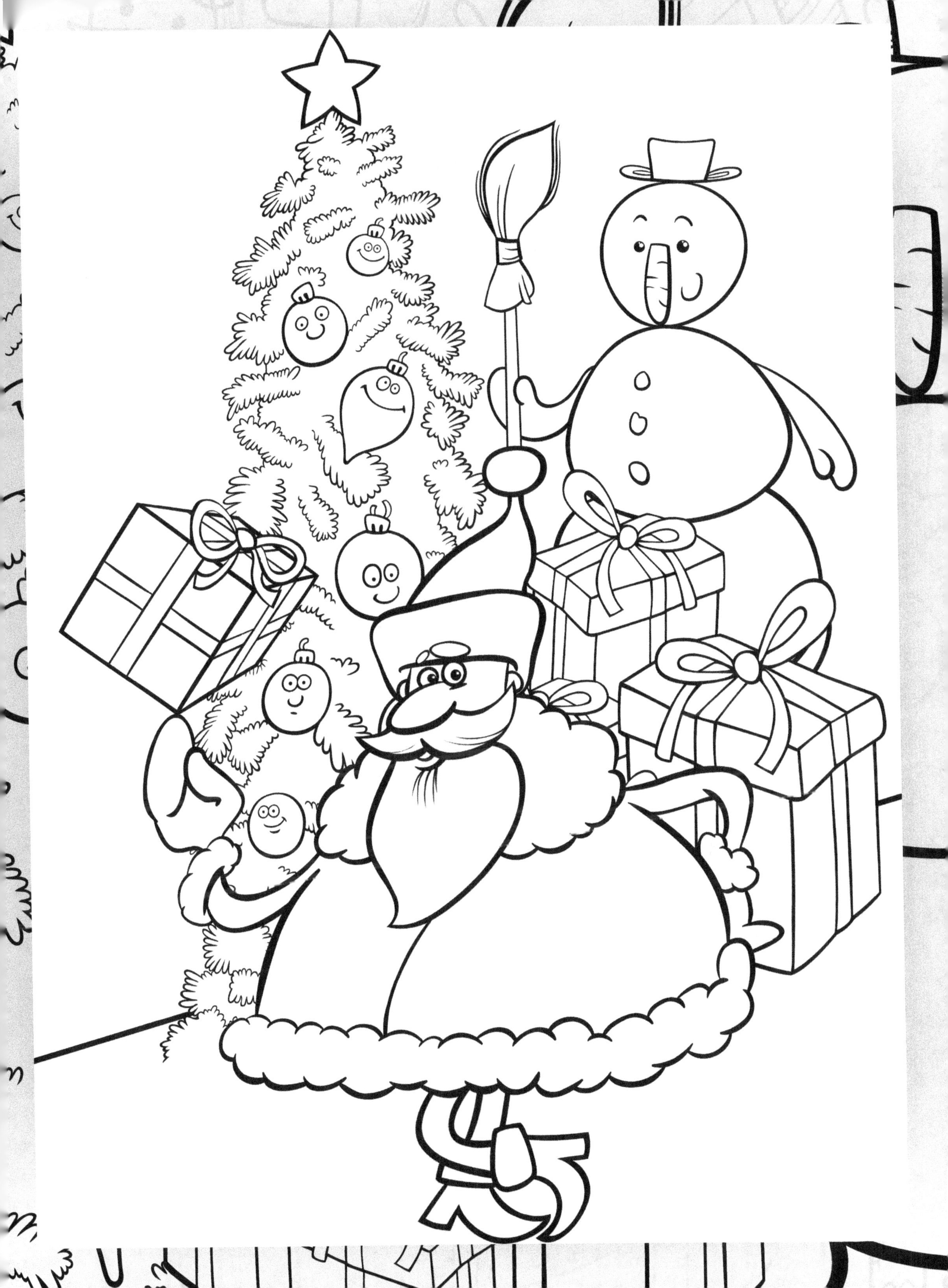

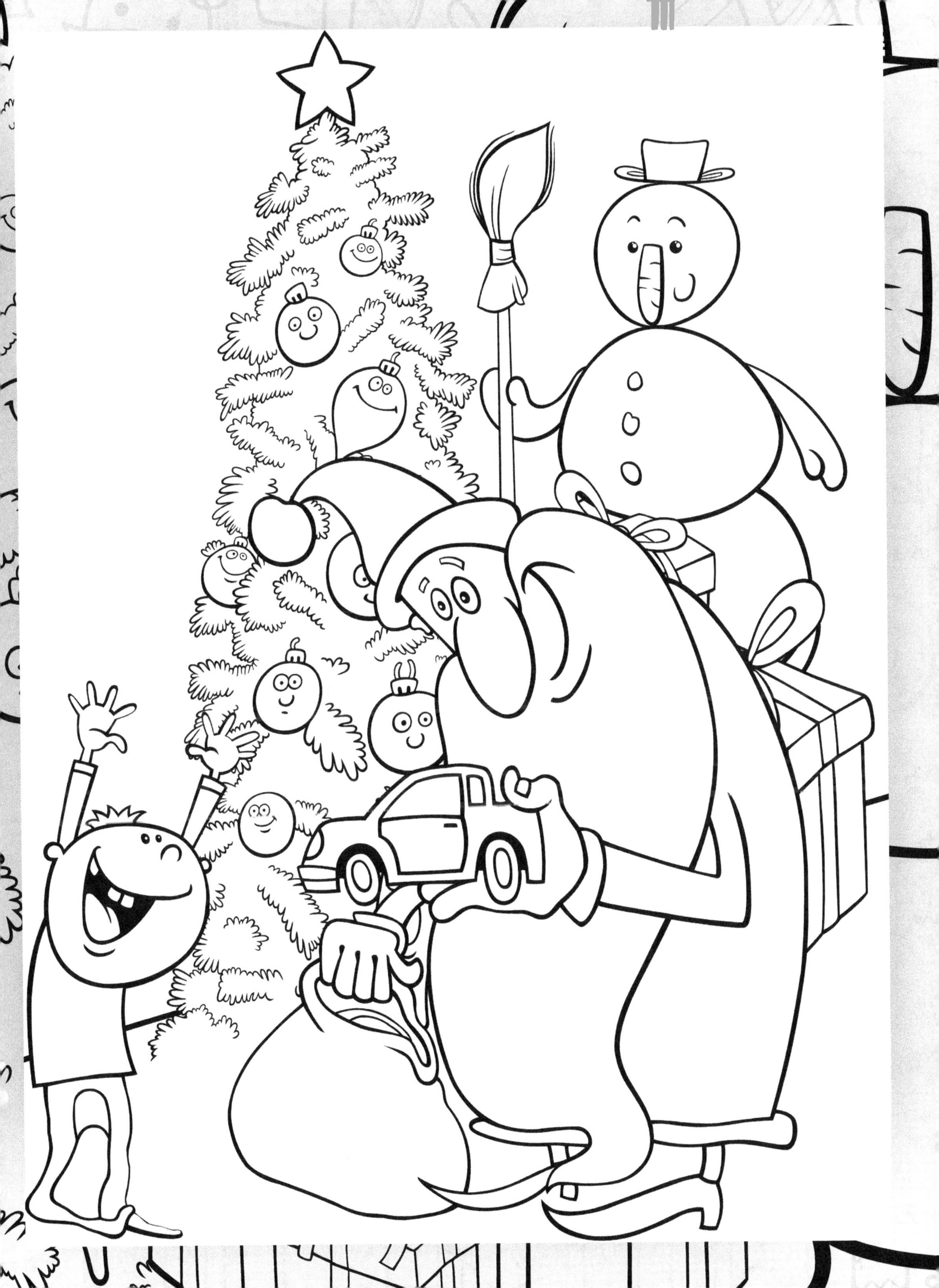

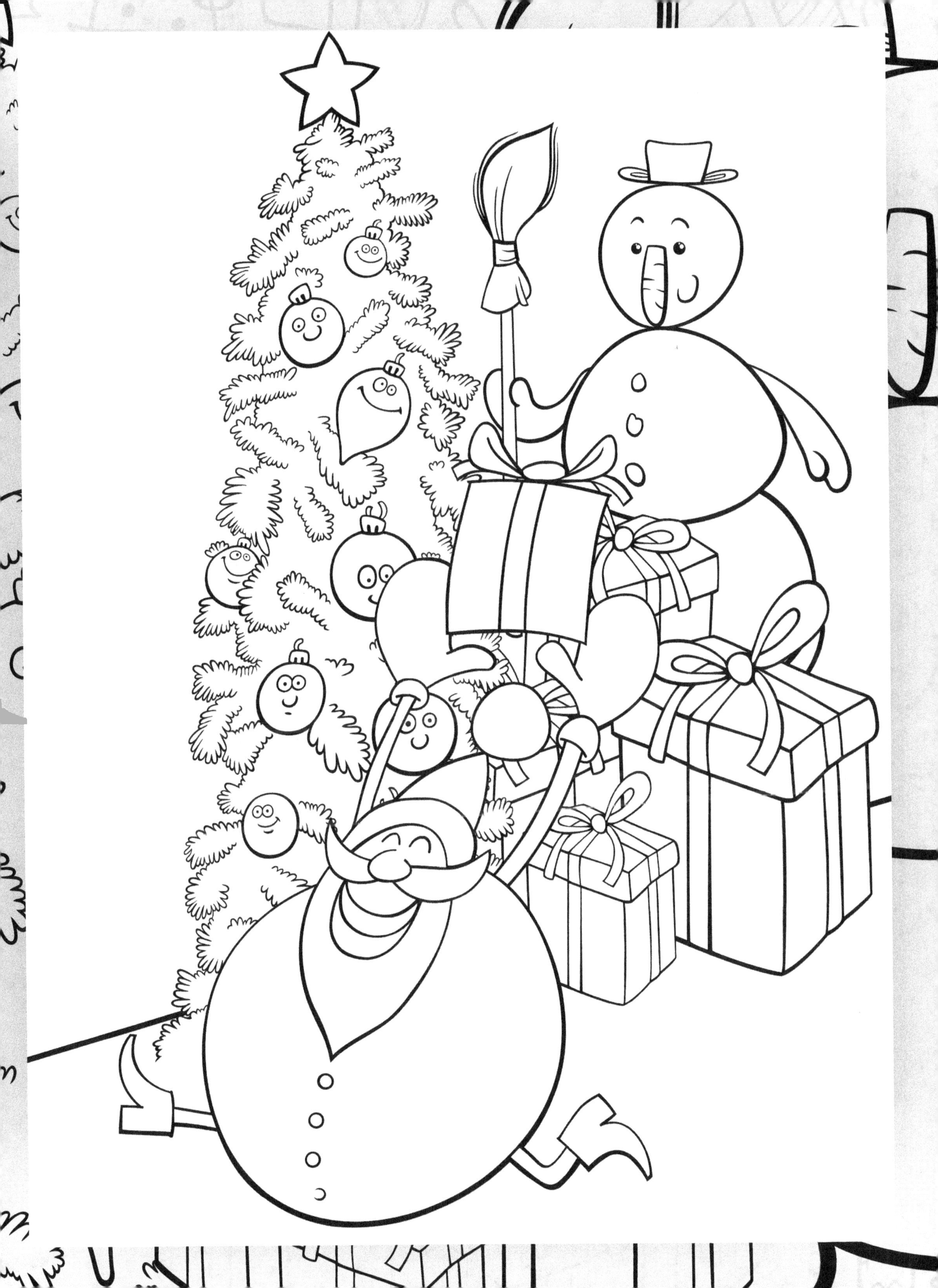

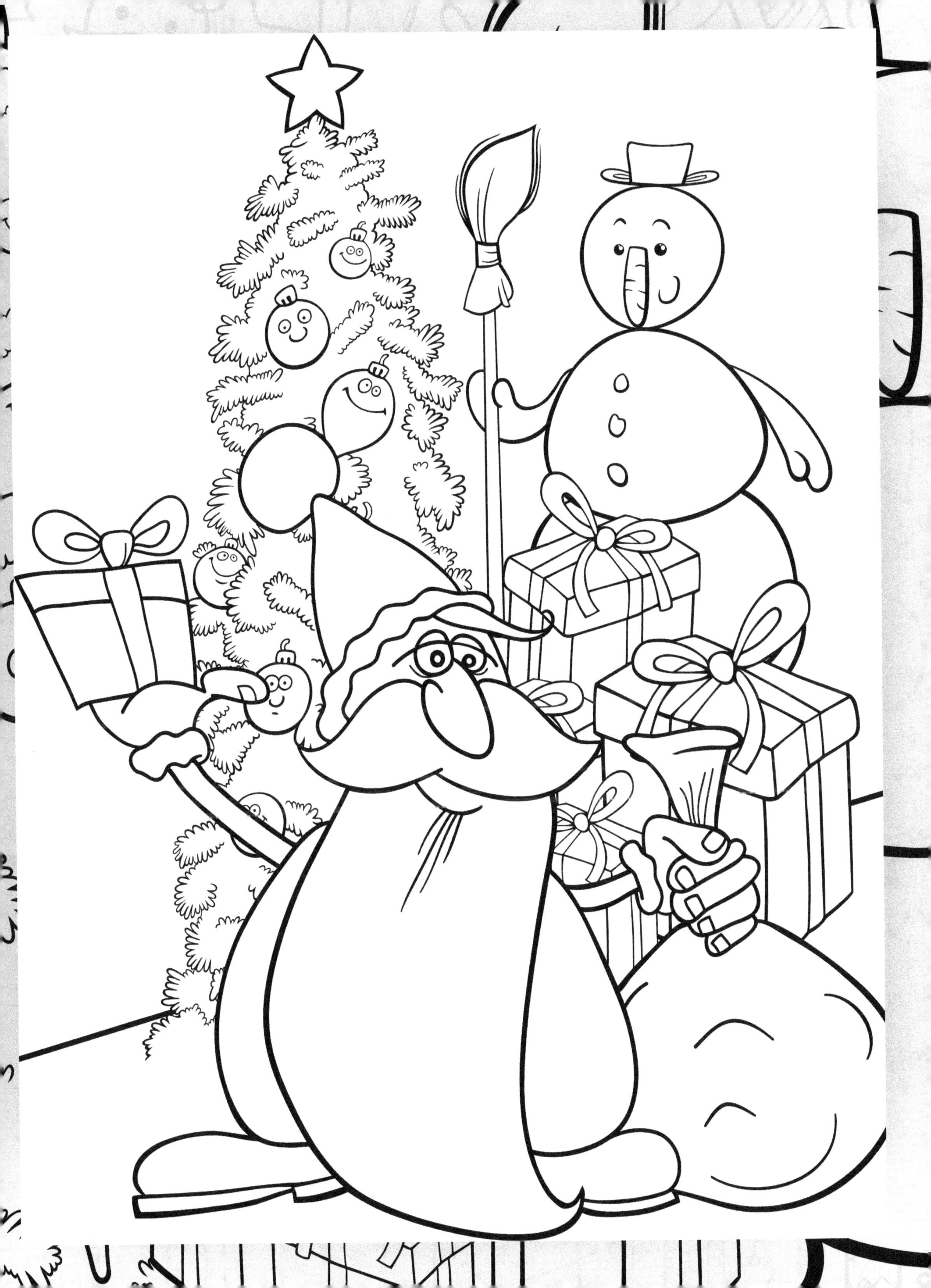

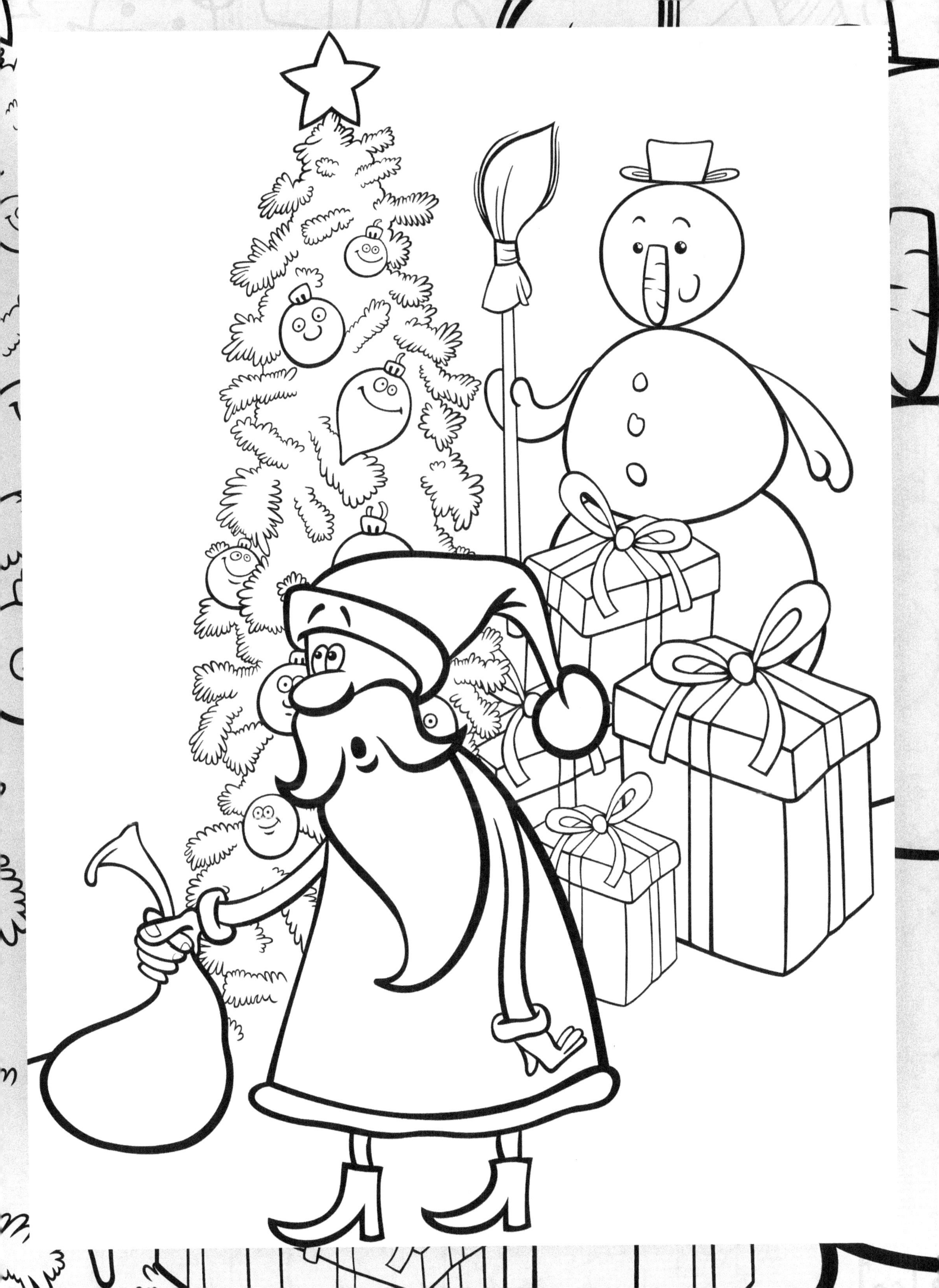

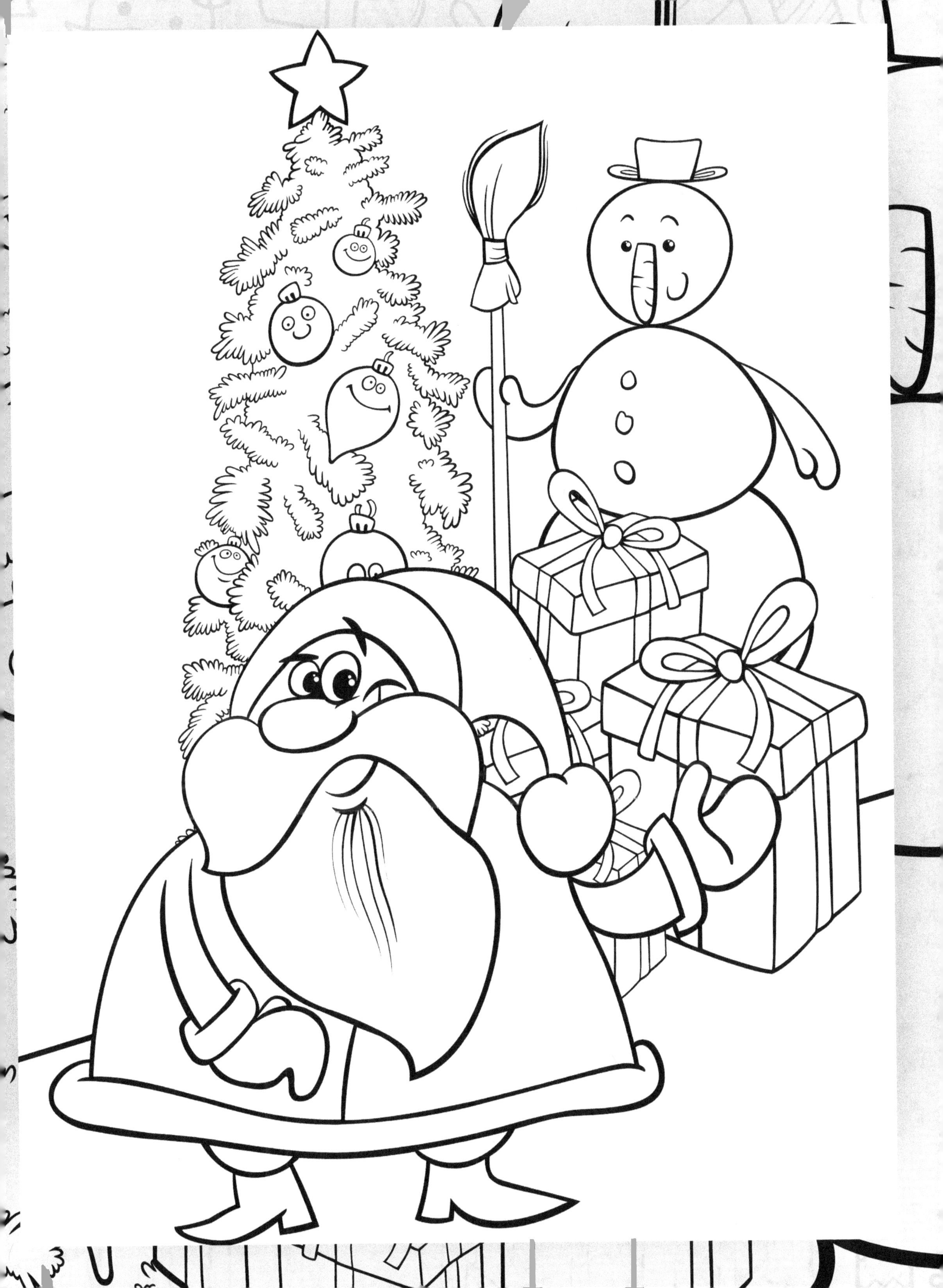

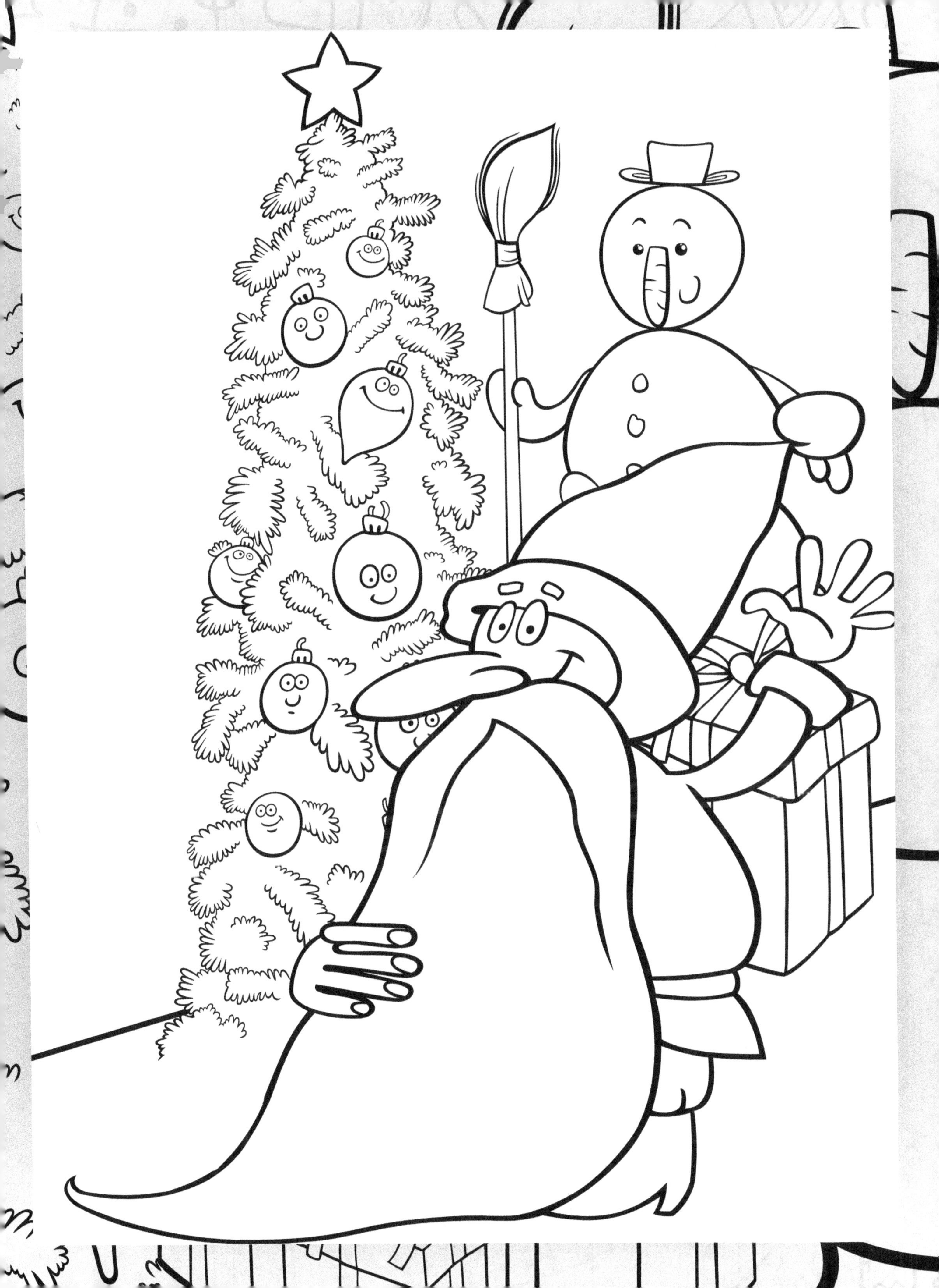

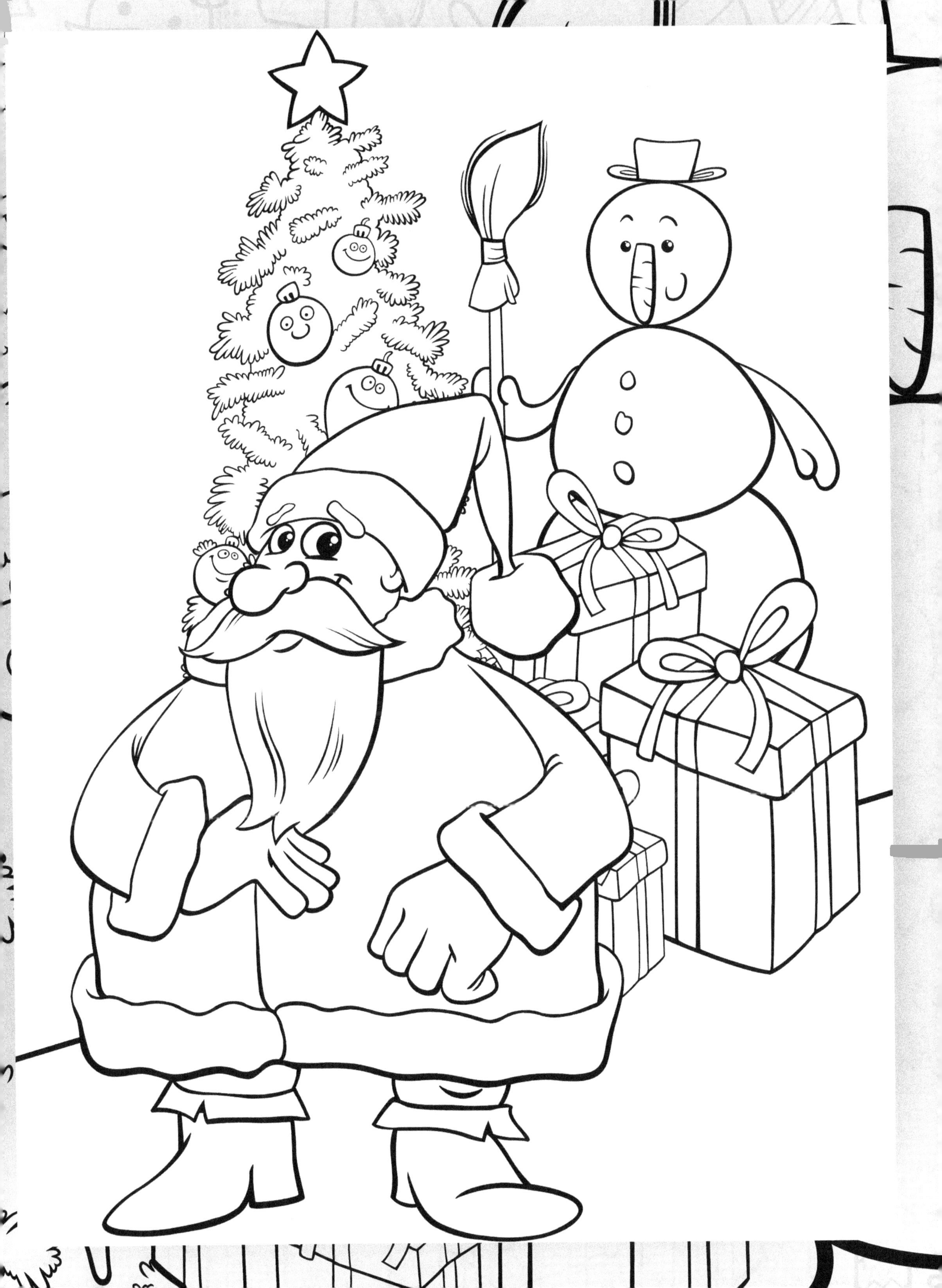

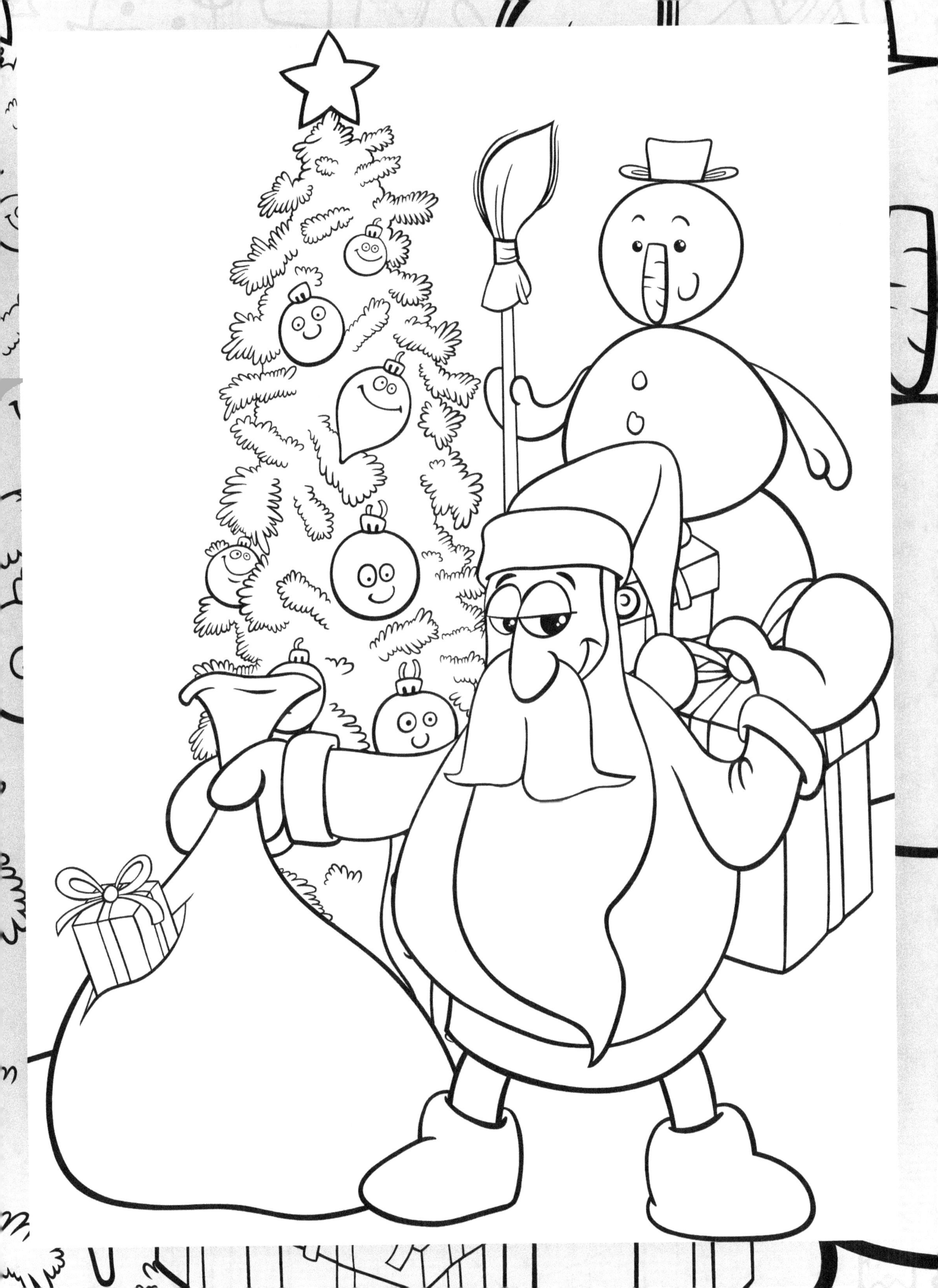

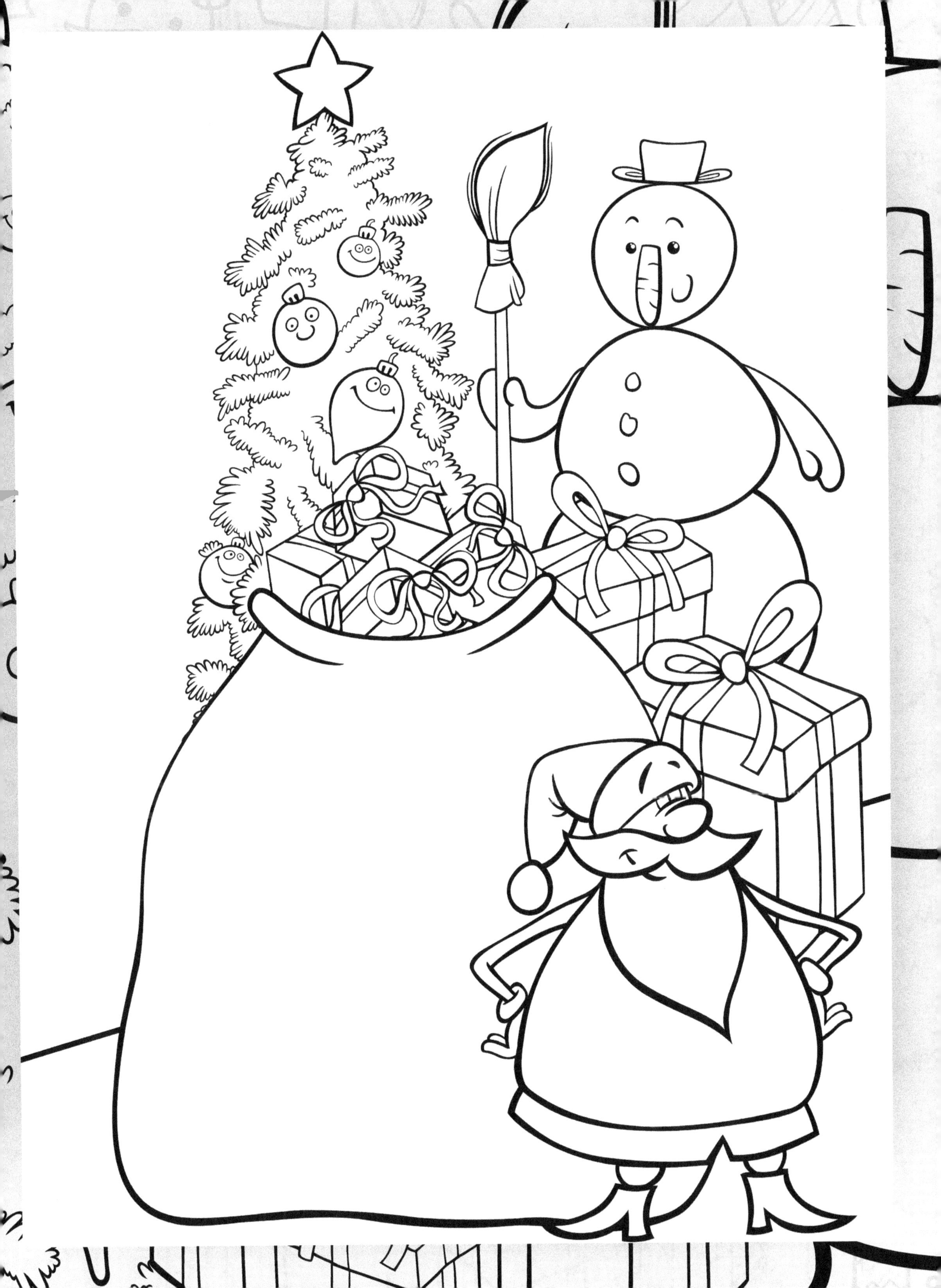

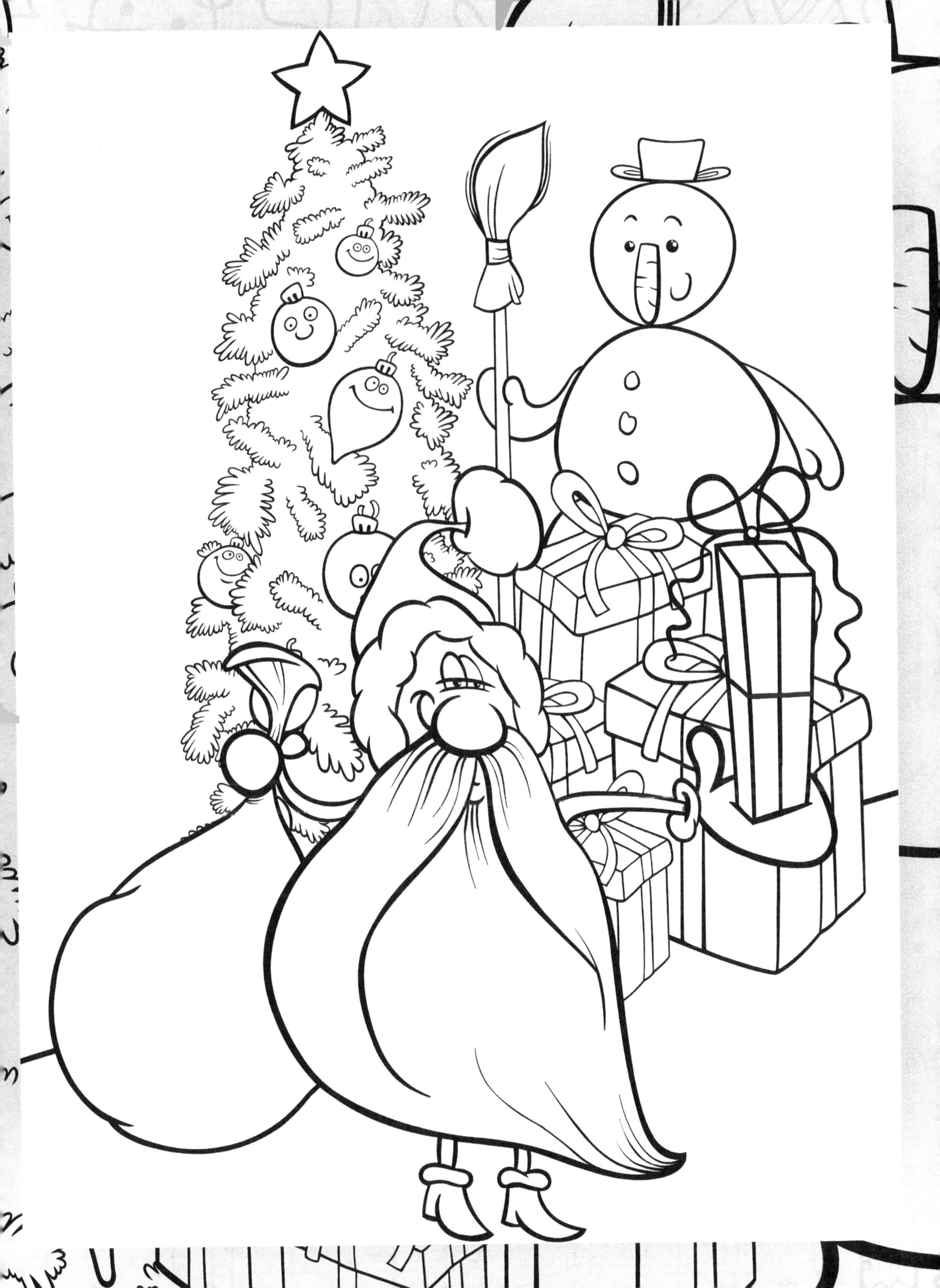

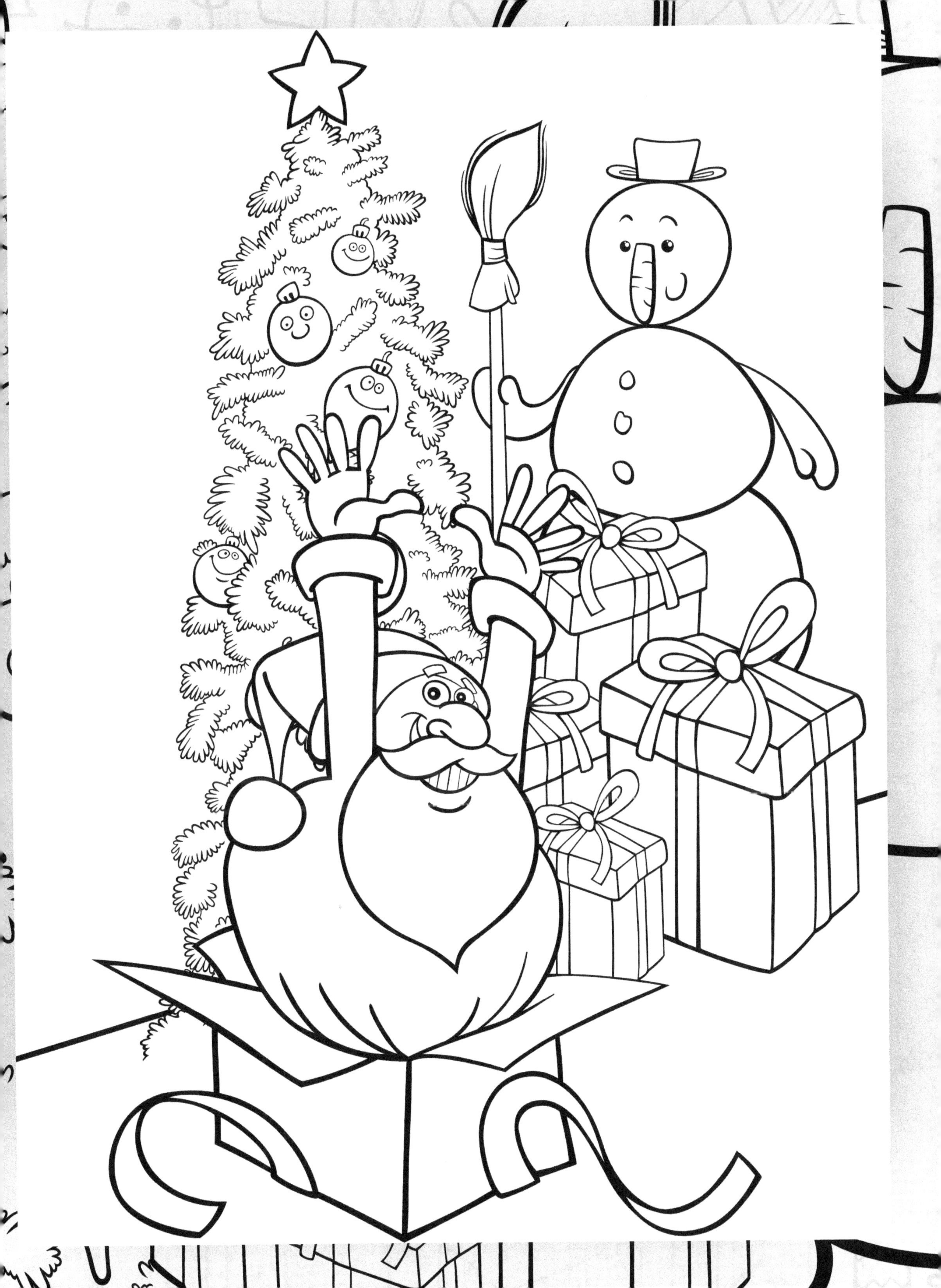

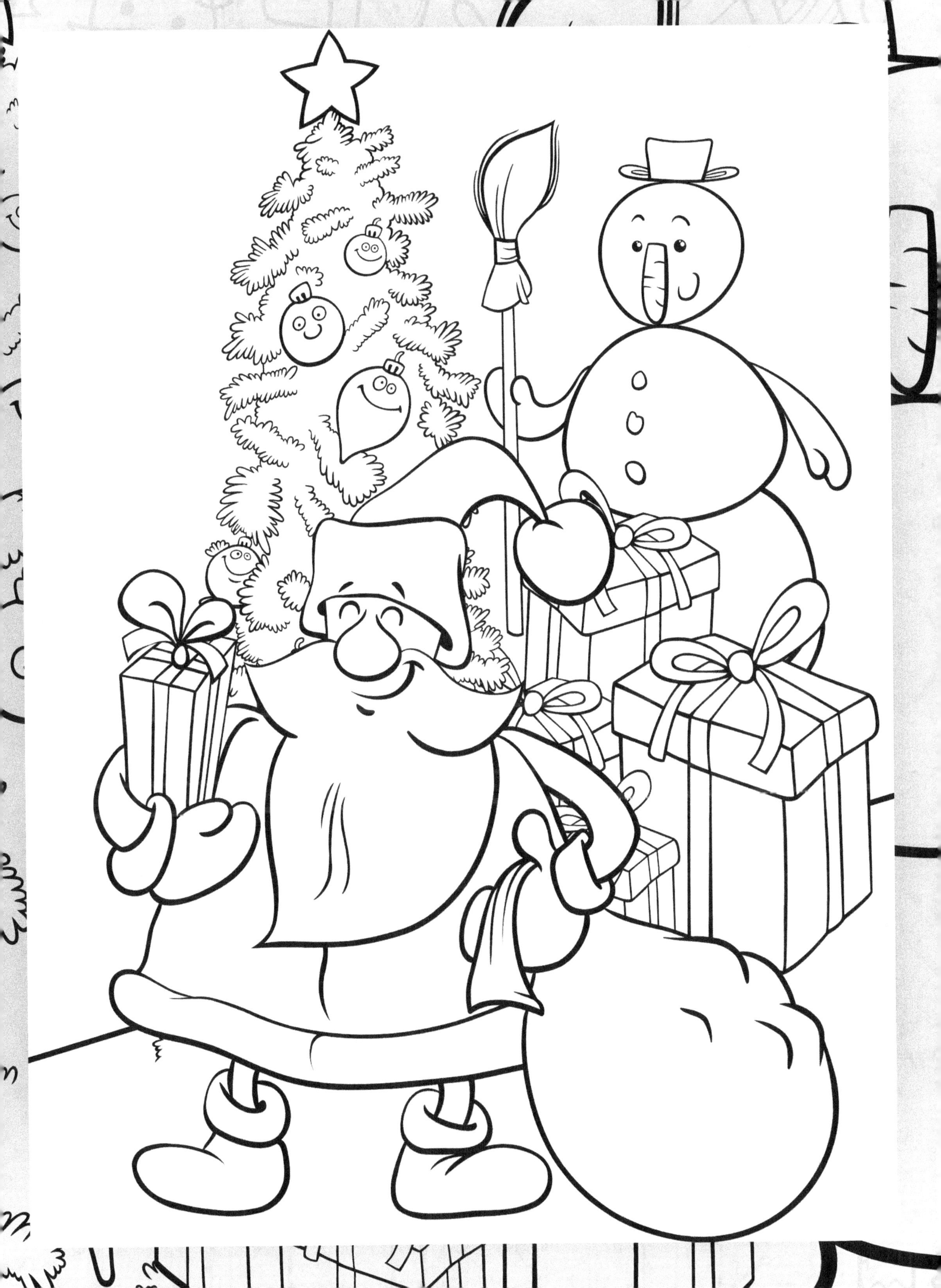

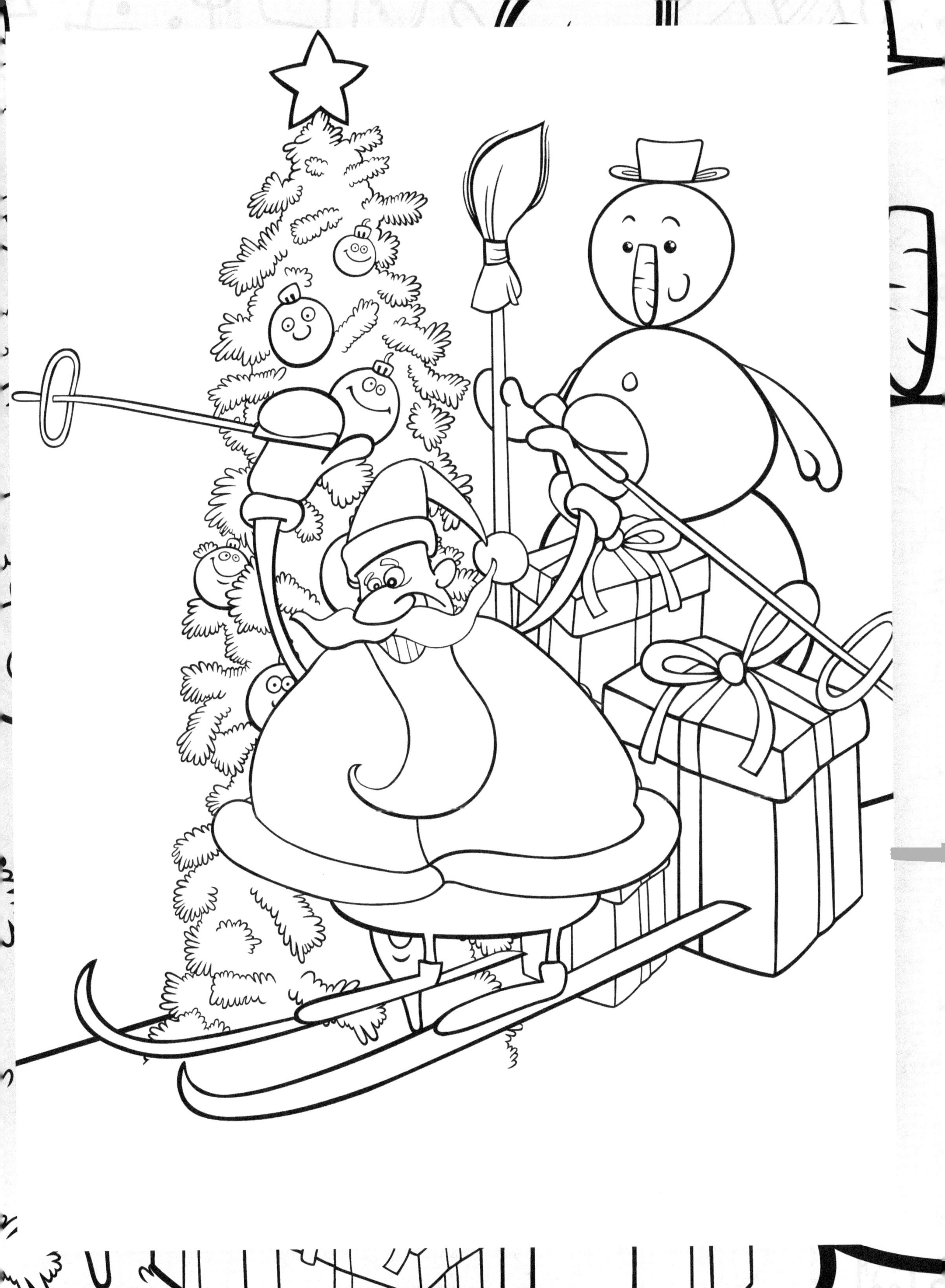

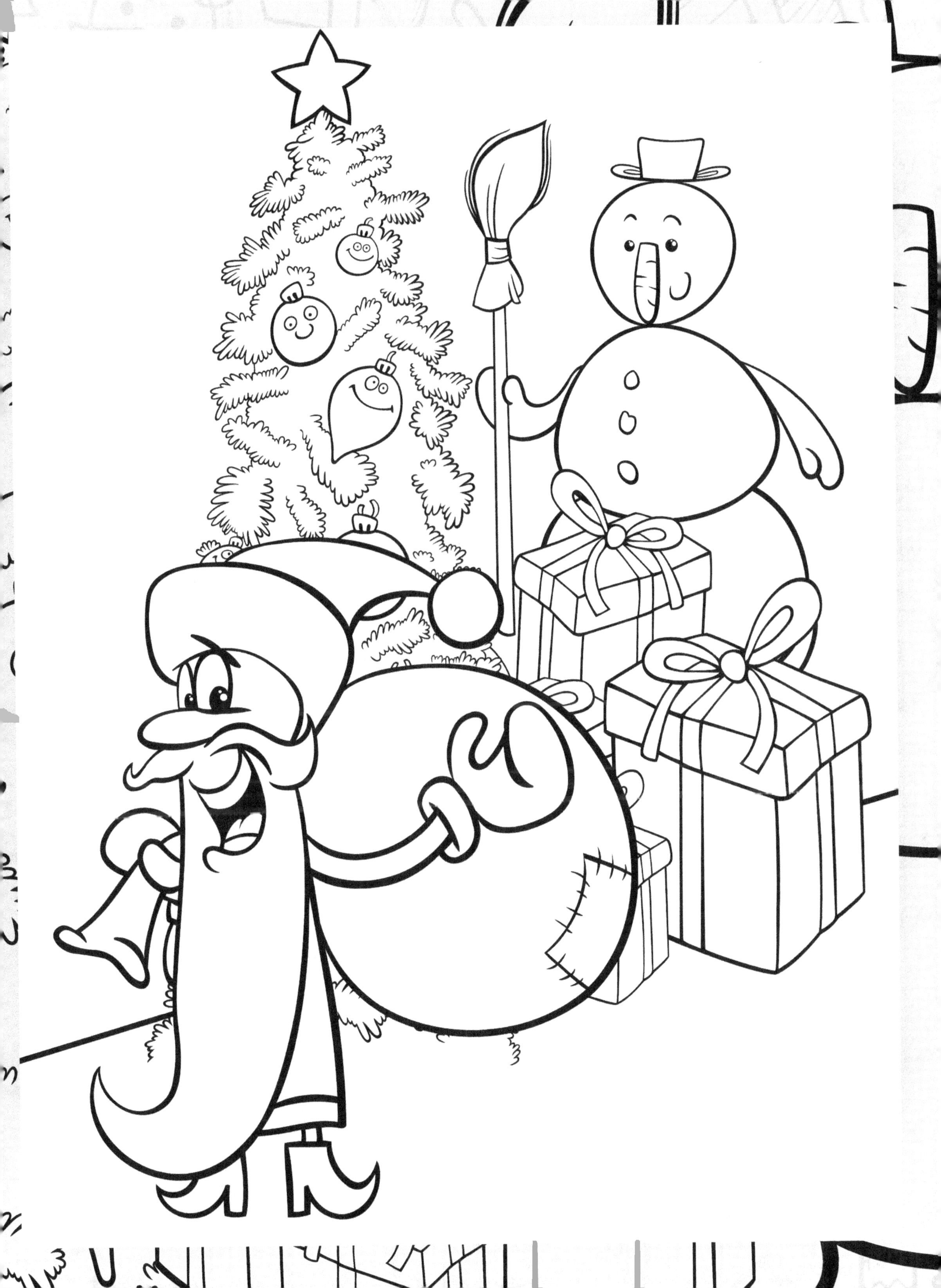

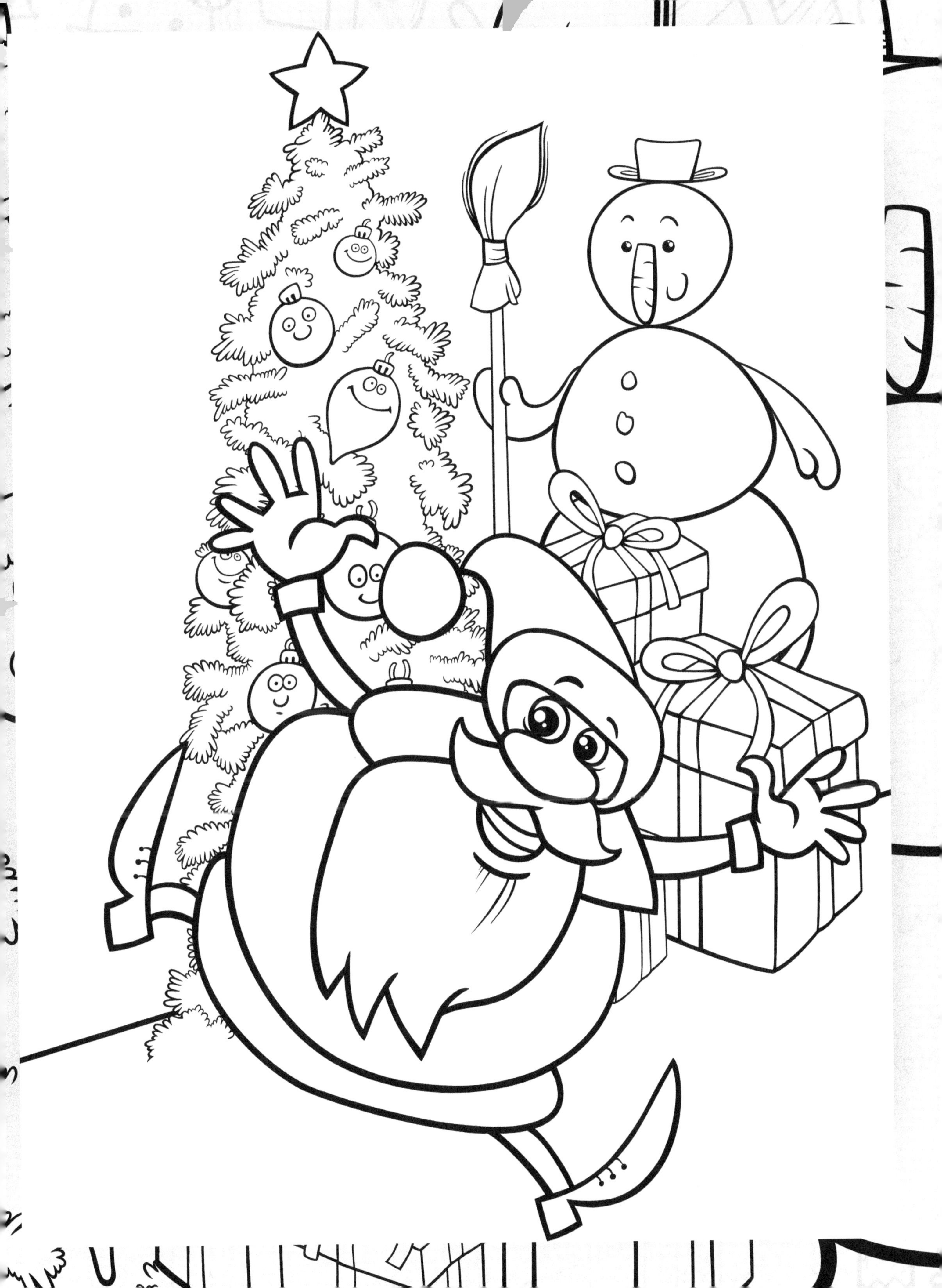

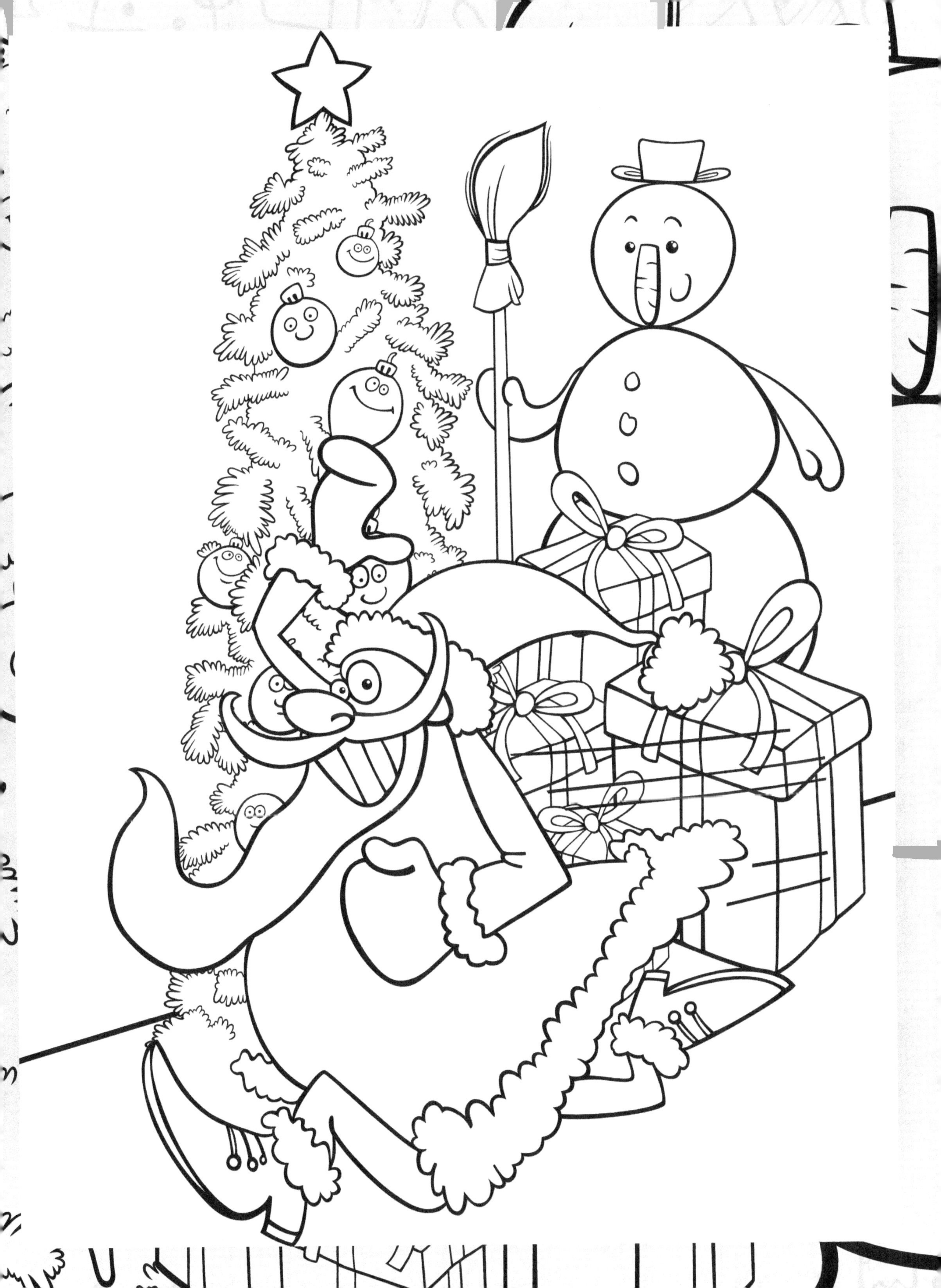

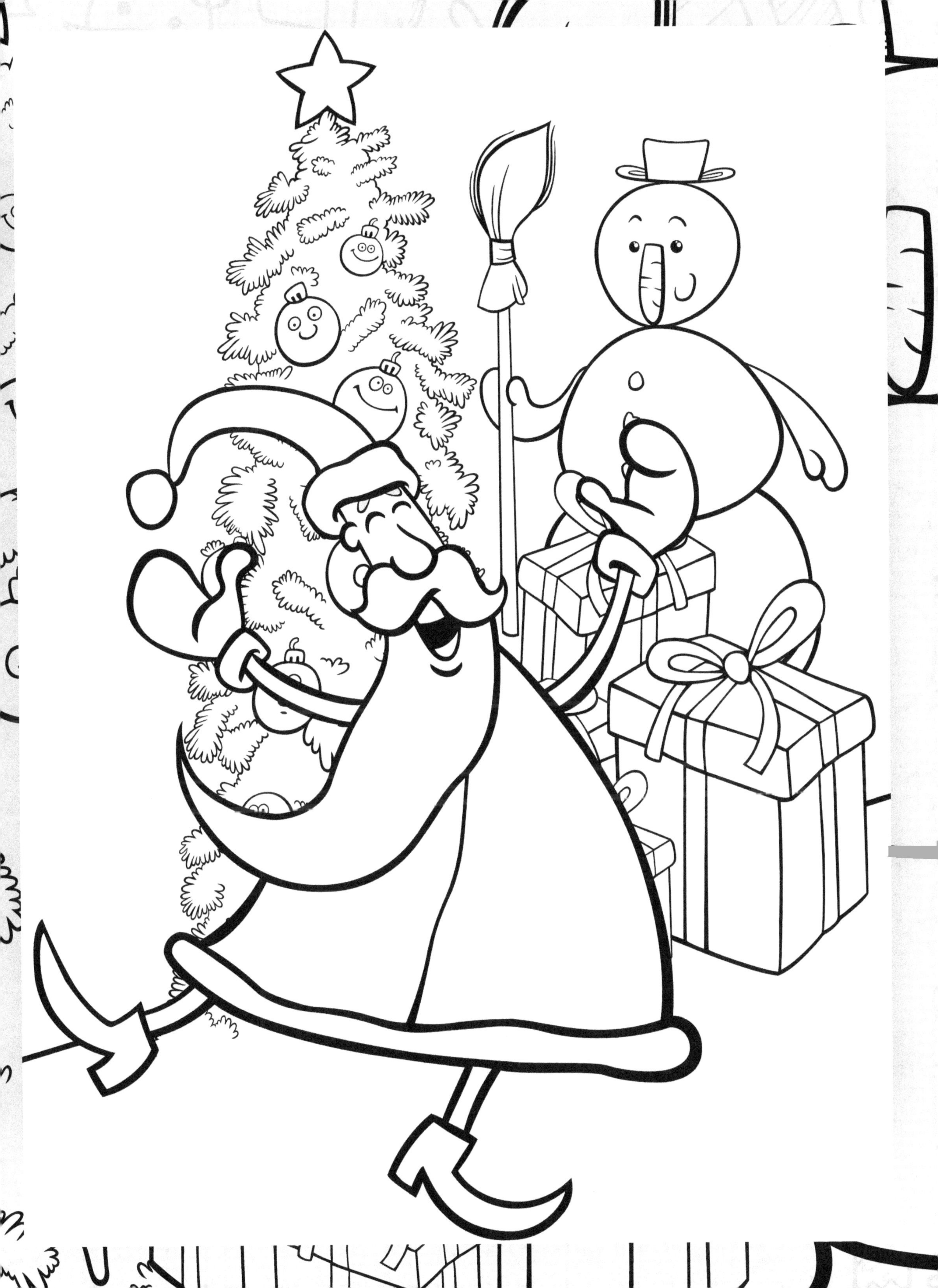

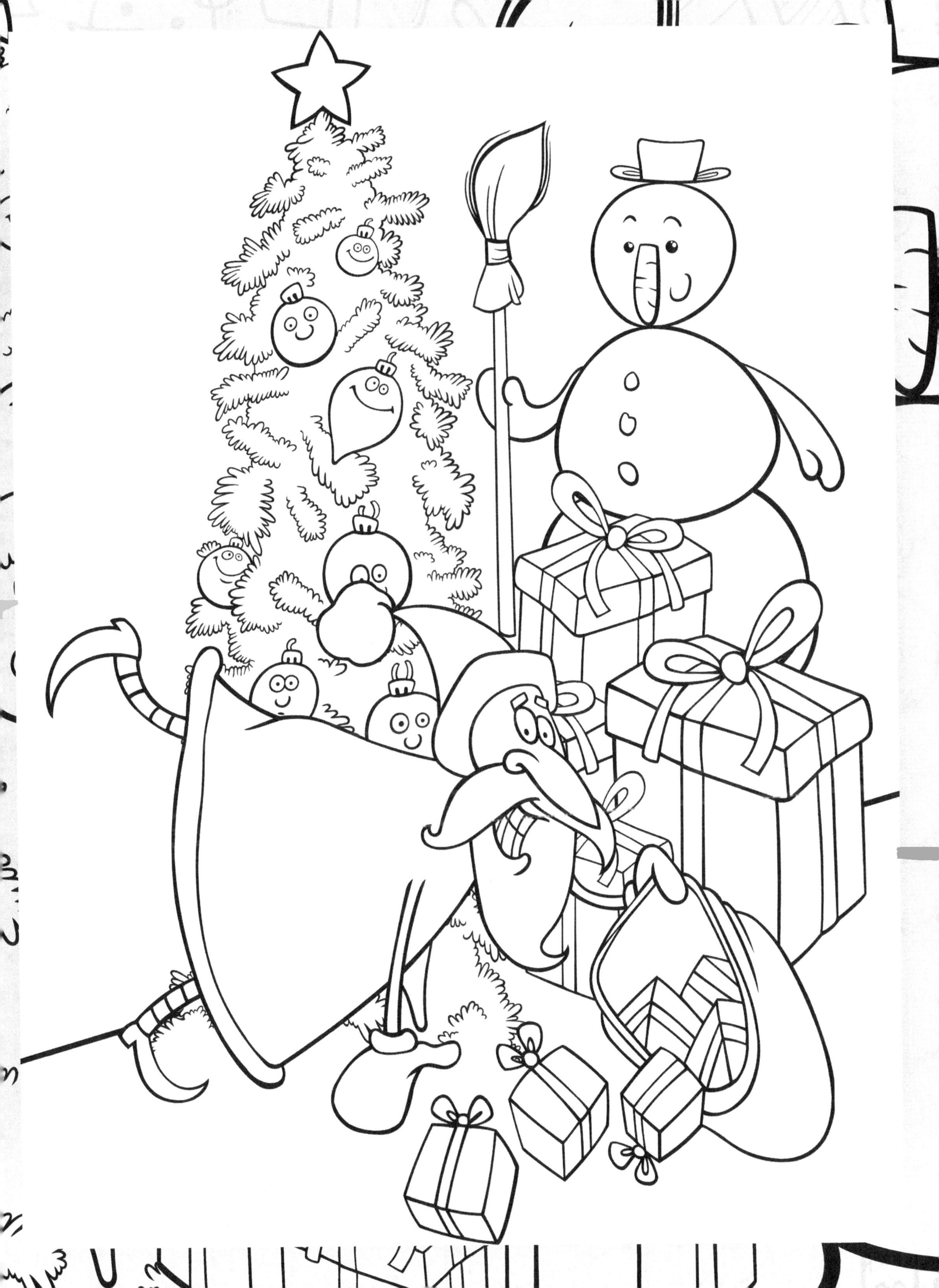

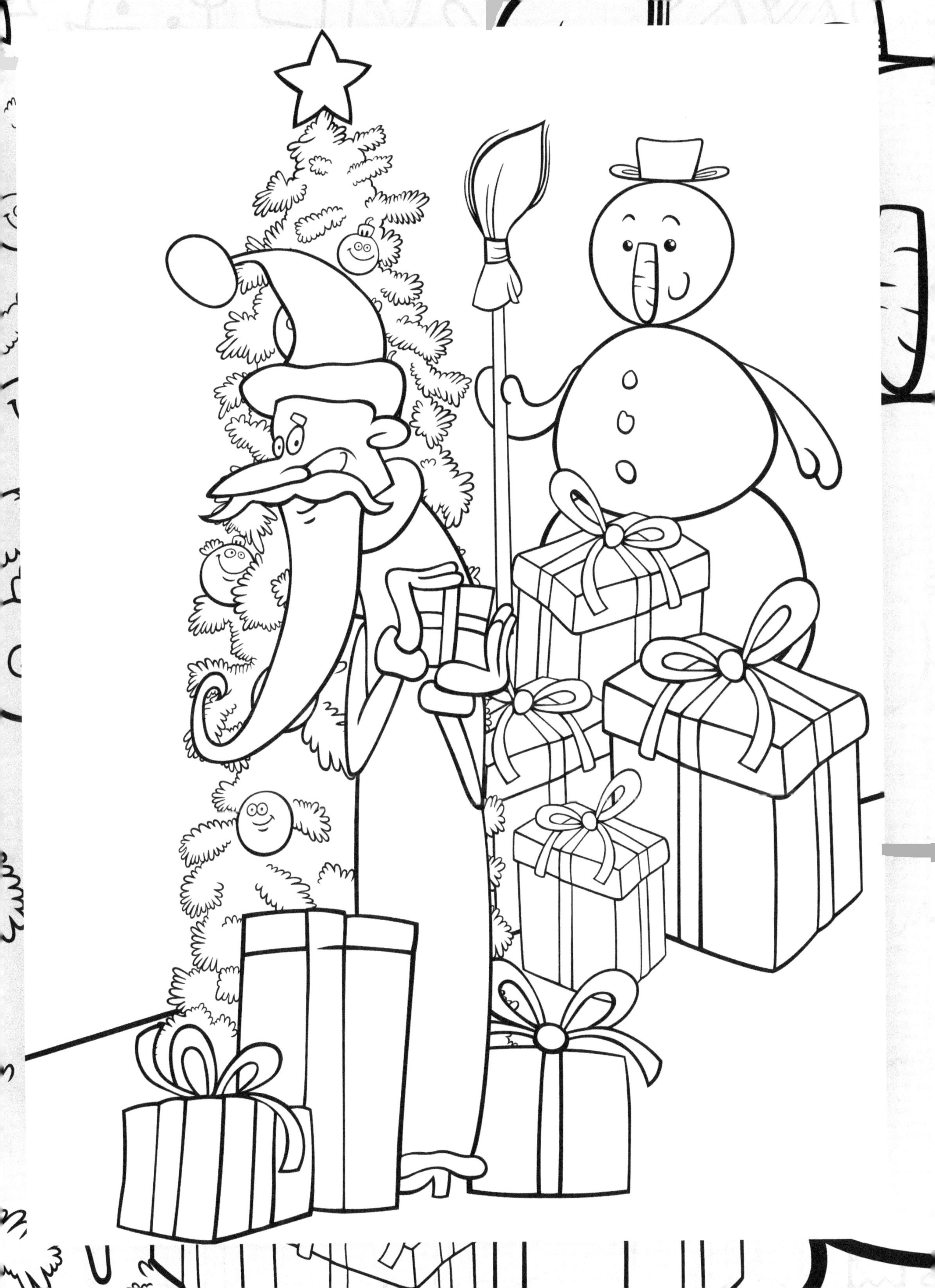

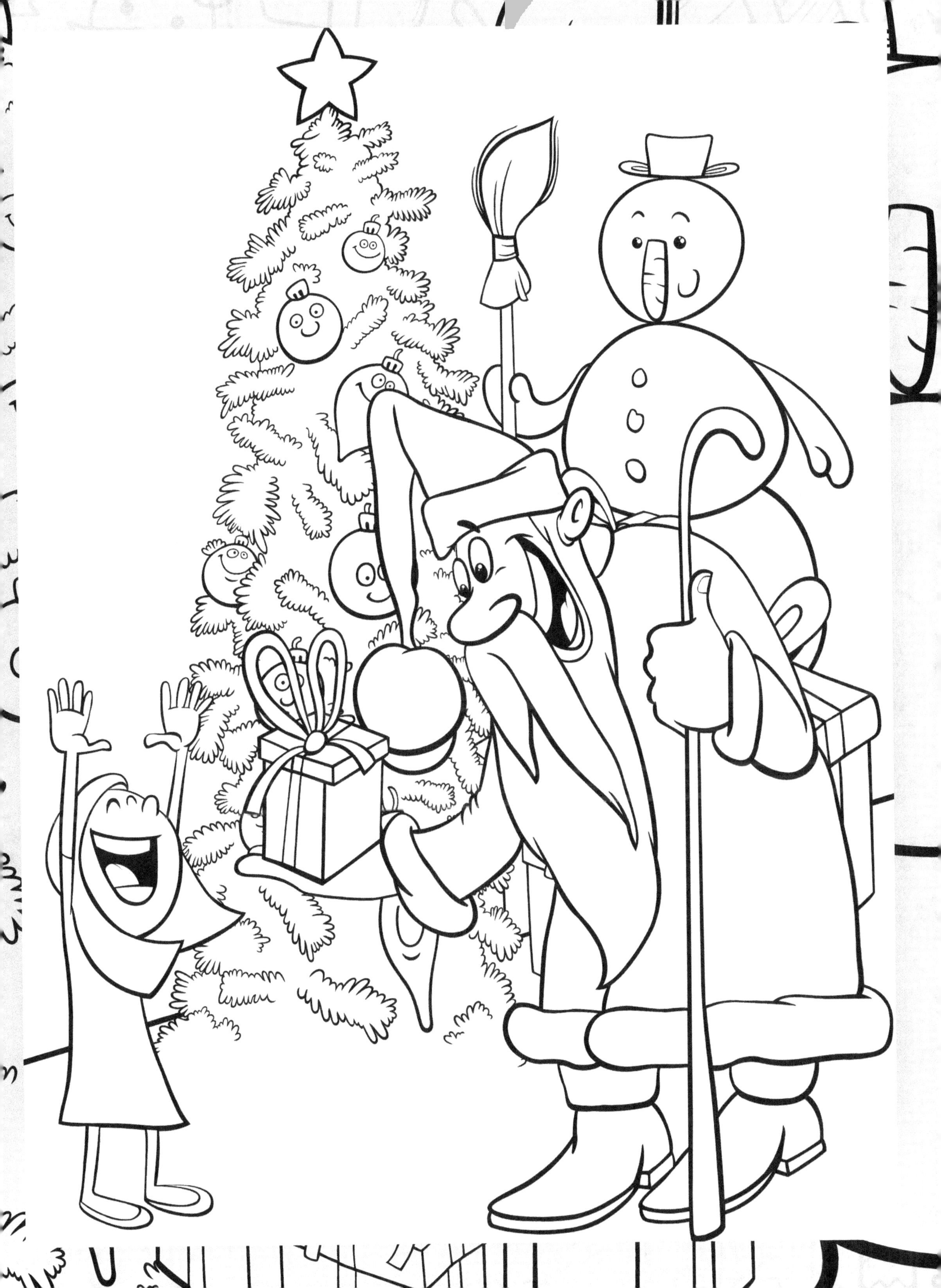

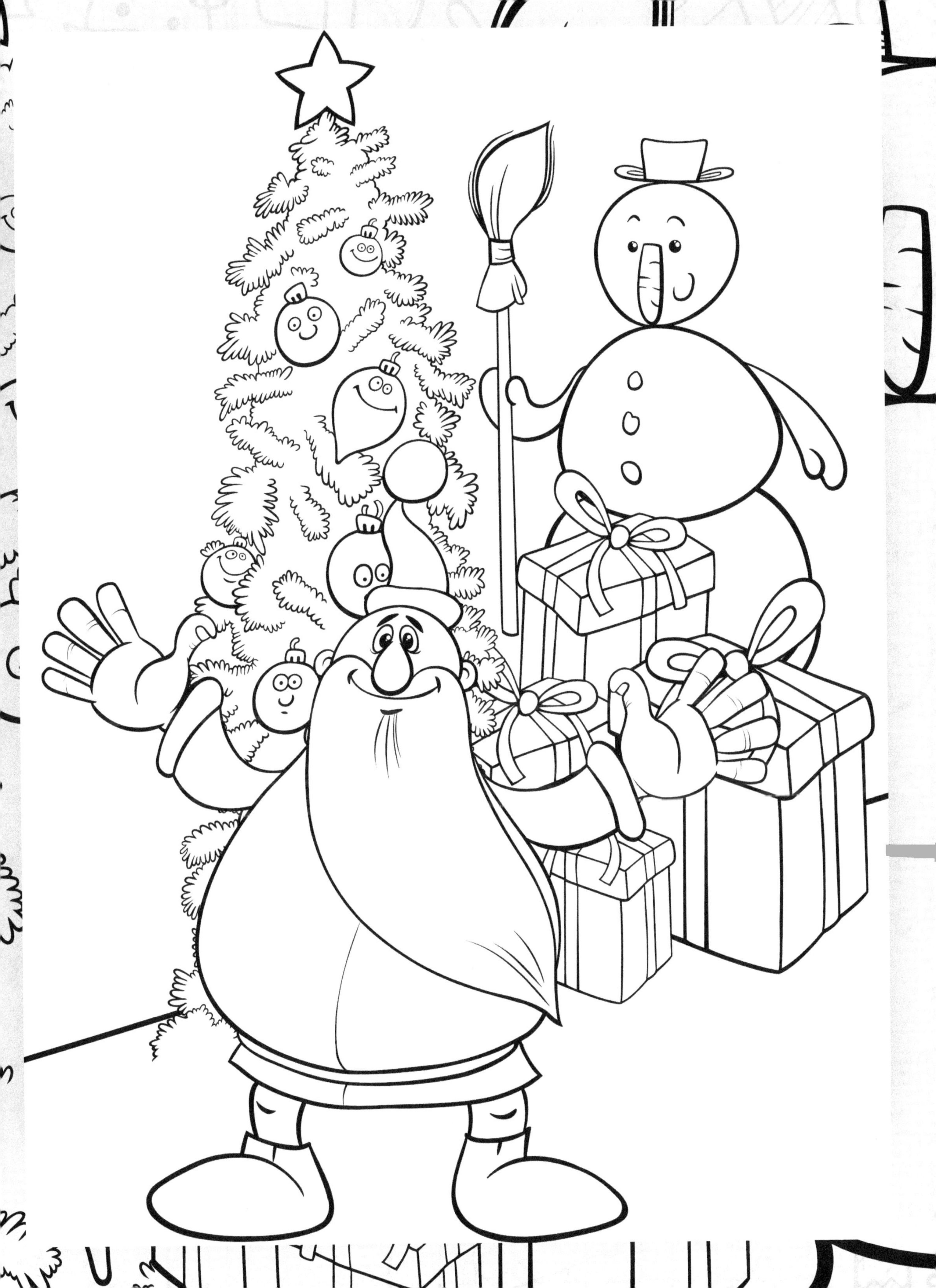

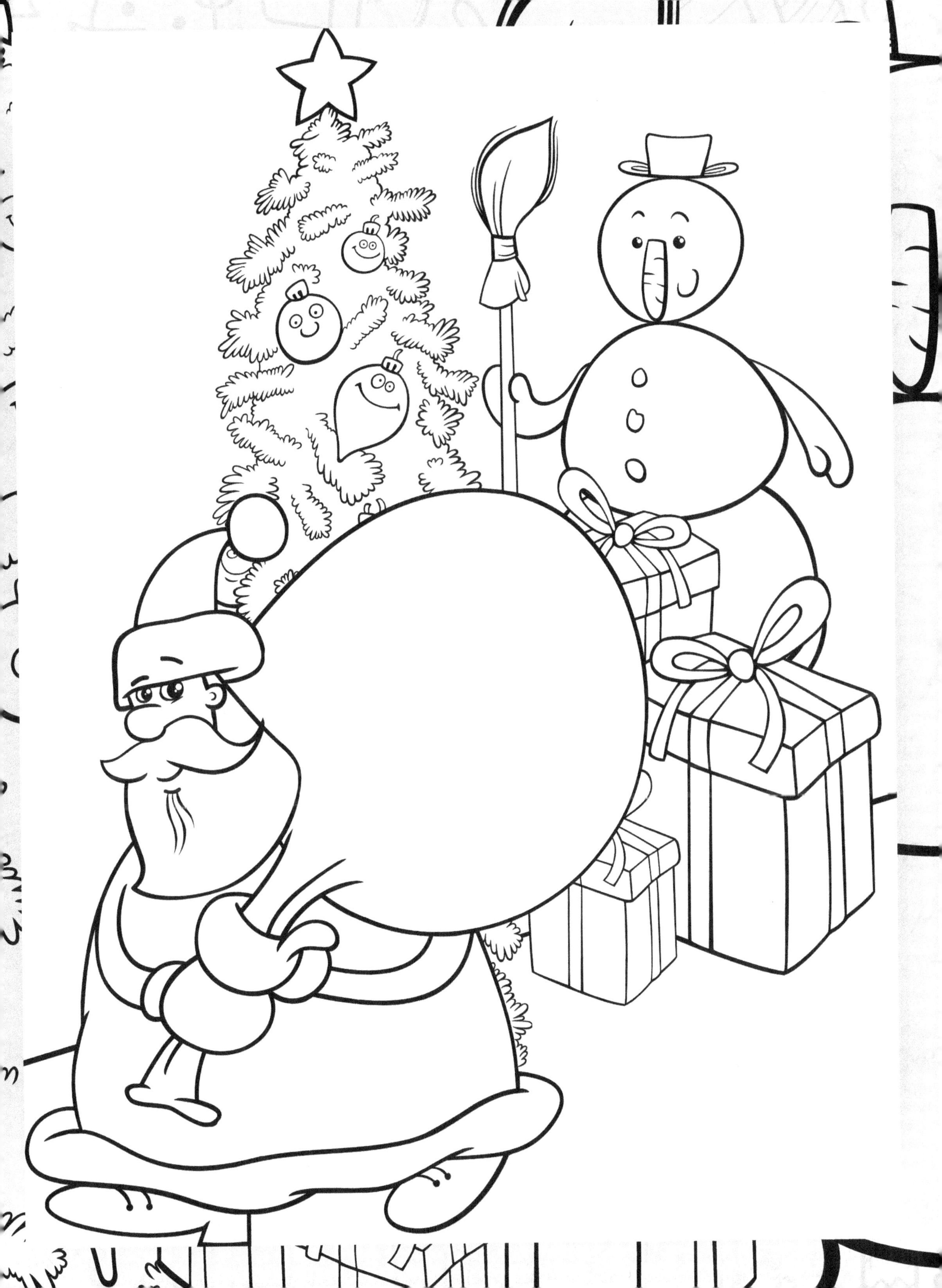

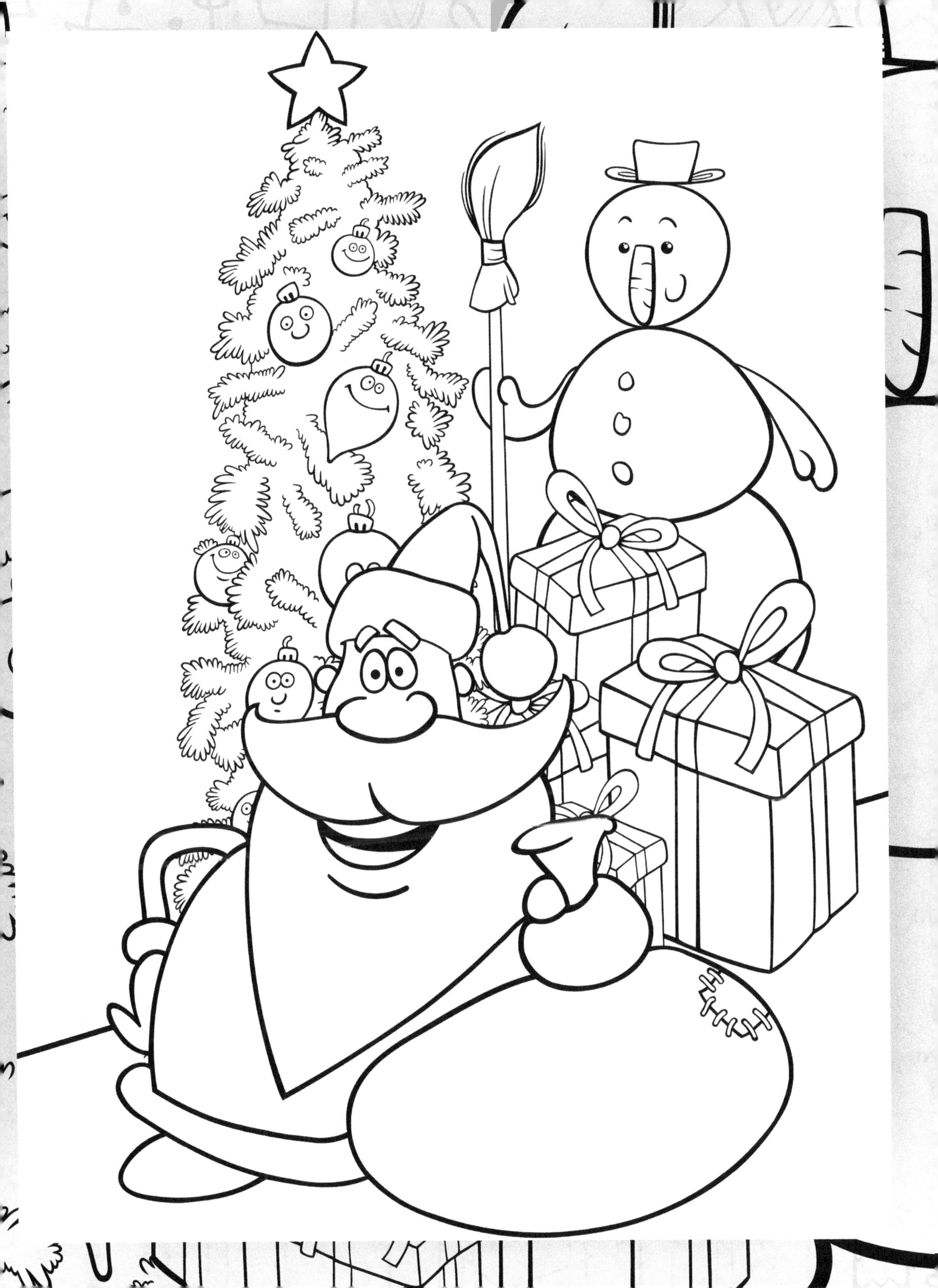